P9-DNZ-515

PRAISE FOR JACQUES PÉPIN AND TODAY'S GOURMET

"In the rarefied world of internationally famous chefs, Pépin is
remarkable for the range of his knowledge and experience."
—*Hartford [CT] Courant*

"This is a cooking show for true foodies that will send
sensualists straight into the kitchen."
—*New York Times*

"Jacques Pépin, one of the world's most famous chefs and cookbook
authors, translates brilliantly to television. The extremely attractive
Pépin, with shirt sleeves rolled up to show muscular forearms,
cooks delicious-sounding healthy dishes. His food is so simple that
it could be recreated by an adventurous cook."
—*St. Louis Post-Dispatch*

"Pépin's principles are straightforward: cooking can be healthy,
fast, easy, and fun. Pépin's menus are eclectic, ranging from traditional
French to Russian and Vietnamese; from festive Sunday-dinner
and special-guest menus to budget fare."
—*Food Arts*

"Pépin's recipes are consistently the best on television.
And he never condescends."
—*San Francisco Examiner*

"Pépin is a master of technique. He never misses an opportunity
to turn a seemingly difficult task into a lesson in simplicity.
Watching him, you'll realize why, when it comes to cooking, the
French get all the glory."
—*Seattle Weekly*

"Jacques Pépin probably has the deftest hands in the business,
but he's right up there in the brains department, too. What he does
better than anyone else is make ordinary dishes delicious."
—*San Francisco Image Magazine*

"Sweet, suave, and silver-haired, Jacques Pépin is the sex symbol
of the cooking show circuit—and perhaps the demi-god under Child.
The French-born author-chef needs no gastronomical gimmicks
to enchant. Pépin's modern French dishes are mouth-watering."
—*New York Daily News*

HAPPY COOKING!

MORE LIGHT CLASSICS FROM
TODAY'S GOURMET

JACQUES PÉPIN

Production of the public television series
Today's Gourmet with Jacques Pépin
is made possible by generous grants from

Braun Inc.
Cambria Winery & Vineyard
Russell Range, Inc.

KQED
BOOKS
SAN FRANCISCO

Publisher:
   Pamela Byers
Production Coordinator and Editor:
   Zipporah W. Collins
Book Designer and
Photography Art Director:
   Barbara Marks
Photographer:
   Penina
Food and Prop Stylist:
   Heidi Gintner
Photography Chef:
   Carl Abbott
Assistants to Jacques Pépin:
   Norma Galehouse
   Tina Salter
Cover Designer:
   Adrian Morgan
Cover Photographer:
   Penina
Illustrations by:
   Jacques Pépin
Props provided by:
   Biordi Art Imports
   Bourgeat USA
   Domestications Catalog
   Macy's California
   Pier 1 Imports
   Pierre Deux
   Saint-Louis Cristal—Hermès Art
      de la Table
   Sakura, Inc.
   Signature China
   Williams-Sonoma

For KQED:
President and CEO:
   Mary G. F. Bitterman
Vice President for Publishing and
New Ventures:
   Mark K. Powelson

© 1994 by Jacques Pépin. First Edition. All rights reserved.
No part of this book may be used or reproduced in any manner whatsoever
without written permission of the publisher except in the case of brief
quotations in critical articles and reviews. For information, address:
KQED, Inc., 2601 Mariposa Street, San Francisco, California 94110.

Library of Congress Cataloging-in-Publication Data
Pépin, Jacques.
         Happy cooking! : more light classics from Today's Gourmet / Jacques
Pépin.
               p.   cm.
         Includes index.
         ISBN 0–912333–27–8
         1. Cookery. 2. Today's gourmet (Television program). I. Today's
gourmet (Television program) II. Title.
TX714.P455 1994
614.5—dc20   94–29076
                                                                         CIP

ISBN 0–912333–27–8

Manufactured in the United States of America

10   9   8   7   6   5   4   3   2   1

Distributed to the trade by Publishers Group West

CONTENTS

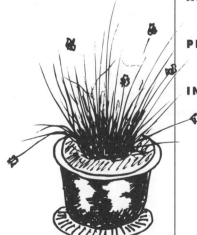

INTRODUCTION

Happy Cooking! presents the same kind of light, flavorful cuisine I introduced in the original *Today's Gourmet* television series and its companion cookbook. The shows, which emphasize a commonsense approach to cooking—the way I cook at home—have been extremely well received, and I thank viewers for their enthusiastic response to both the series and the books.

The recipes in this book reflect my style of life and the importance of food, which is tightly interwoven into the context of my family life as well as countless gatherings with friends. Food is the common denominator that brings people together in my house, and this is evidenced in the recipes that follow.

You'll see that health also concerns me greatly. Although *Happy Cooking!* is not intended to be a dietetic, low-calorie, low-fat, low-sodium, or low-cholesterol book, the recipes here reflect how important I think good nutrition is, along with seasonal ingredients and fresh food. Yet keep in mind that I am a cook, not a doctor. Eating, for me, has always meant enjoyment and sharing, never prohibitions.

In these pages, I want to introduce you to a cuisine that demonstrates a rational approach to cooking. It is a sensitive and sensible way to cook, a cooking style that emphasizes aspects of health in a commonsense way—a diverse diet with more fiber and less saturated fat, more fish and shellfish, smaller portions of well-trimmed meat, vegetables cooked in a manner that preserves vitamins and nutrients—and still a cooking style full of elegance and joy. This is the cuisine of today and of tomorrow; it represents a lower-calorie, healthier, more modern, faster, and simpler way of cooking.

This kind of cooking avoids gimmicks and trends; rather, it satisfies the tastes of a discriminating audience while meeting their nutritional needs in a nonprescriptive way. I want a cuisine that appeals to the epicurean and the jogger as well as the busy home cook and the single professional. Some of the recipes are simple, lending themselves well to family meals; others, containing richer ingredients, are more elaborate, better suited to parties.

In the "happy cooking" I do, I also want to show you how proper cooking techniques can save time and effort, so that cooking is more enjoyable. You should have fun in the kitchen and then emerge from it with flavorful, wholesome, attractive dishes that you can serve to both family and guests. My cuisine is not a complicated or contrived mix of esoteric ingredients, and it is not intended for an elite group of people. It is for everyone.

Finally, I want to show the importance of togetherness, conviviality, and *joie de vivre* in the kitchen. Cooking should be exciting—nothing compares to the enjoyment of sharing food while spending time with family and friends! But, most of all, I hope that the knowledge readers gain from *Happy Cooking!* will make their lives richer, healthier, and more enjoyable.

ACKNOWLEDGMENTS

Production of the third season of *Today's Gourmet* and this companion cookbook featuring the recipes I demonstrated was an exciting experience that demanded a great deal of teamwork on the part of many capable people. I would like to thank the people associated with all aspects of this project for their help and support. Although it is impossible to name everyone, I especially want to thank:

Peter Stein, my able executive producer, who has become a good friend over the five years we've worked together; *Peggy Lee Scott,* my producer, whose stamina, good disposition, constant smile, and generous advice inspired us all; *Tina Salter,* associate producer, who created the perfect bond between the back kitchen and the set, and understood me so well that she could block my movements perfectly; *June Ouellette,* associate producer, who cheerfully and efficiently managed all the nitty-gritty details behind the scenes; *Leslee Newcomb,* makeup artist, who helped me "lose" all those years; *Katherine Zilavy,* assistant to the producer, whose great work on the computer produced clear instructions for us all; *Katherine Russell,* director, and *Linda Giannecchini,* assistant director, for beautiful close-ups of the food and for following all my moves; *Harry Betancourt, Brad Cochrane, Greg Overton,* and *Mike Ratusz,* the dedicated camera operators, for their great collective "eye"; *Greg King,* who ably operated the remote camera; *Margaret Clarke* and *Jim Summers,* floor directors, for their professionalism and giving me the proper cues on time; *Greg Swartz,* production manager, for my beautiful new counter; and *Jolee Hoyt,* unit manager, for paying all the bills.

I am most grateful to the back kitchen staff, whose help was indispensable to the success of this season of shows: *Carl Abbott,* affable back kitchen manager and chef, and his incredible team, among them *Michelle Royston,* who took me marketing and ran countless errands; *Bernice Chuck Fong,* who happily helped where needed; *Mike Pleiss,* always so reliable; *Joseph Strebler,* for his great bread; and *Christine Swett, Dan Trudeau,* and *Christine Wolf,* for their excellent work and devotion. I also want to thank *Bernie Schimbke,* who decorated yet another beautiful kitchen set for me; *Heidi Gintner,* food stylist, and her assistant, *Lorraine Battle,* who produced beautifully tasteful tables, and *Carol Ceresa,* nutritional consultant, whose precise notes helped me give valuable health information to our audience.

I am most pleased that three very special people in my life joined me on a few of the shows this season. Thanks to my daughter, *Claudine,* for cooking with me; my wife, *Gloria,* for finally agreeing to appear with me on camera, and for supporting me through the years; and my good friend *Jean-Claude Szurdak,* who not only gave me a hand on one of the shows but helped out with the food behind the scenes as well.

For their fine work on this companion book, I want to thank:

Pamela Byers, publisher, whose professionalism we all appreciated and found beneficial; *Zipporah Collins,* production coordinator and editor, for her flawless attention to detail; *Barbara Marks,* book designer and art director, whose beautiful layout and sense of style I truly appreciate; *Penina,* photographer, who made the food look terrific and took a great cover photo; and, of course, *Norma Galehouse,* my longtime assistant, for her complete dedication and talent.

—JACQUES PÉPIN

MENUS

ON THE FOLLOWING PAGES I LIST THE TWENTY-SIX MENUS THAT ARE FEATURED ON MY CURRENT TELEVISION SERIES, *TODAY'S GOURMET WITH JACQUES PÉPIN*. ANY RECIPE GROUPING IS ARBITRARY, INFLUENCED BY SUCH FACTORS AS MARKET AVAILABILITY AND PERSONAL FOOD PREFERENCES.

USE MY MENUS MERELY AS A POINT OF DEPARTURE. REORGANIZE AS YOU WISH, TAKING A RECIPE FROM ONE MENU AND ADDING IT TO ANOTHER.

ALTHOUGH THERE ARE ONLY A FEW SALAD RECIPES IN THE BOOK, YOU'LL NOTE THAT I HAVE LISTED SALADS ON MOST OF MY MENUS. WE EAT SALADS EVERY DAY, AND I RECOMMEND THEM FOR TASTE AND BALANCE IN A DIET. BREAD AND WINE ARE ALSO PART OF OUR DAILY FARE. IF YOU INCLUDE THEM WITH YOUR MEALS AS WELL, REMEMBER TO TAKE INTO ACCOUNT THE CALORIES THEY ADD.

WE DON'T EAT DESSERTS ON A REGULAR BASIS AT MY HOUSE, PREFERRING TO END OUR MEALS WITH FRESH FRUITS. I HAVE INCLUDED DESSERT RECIPES HERE, HOWEVER, TO COMPLETE THE MENUS AND MAKE THEM SPECIAL ENOUGH FOR OCCASIONS WHEN YOU ENTERTAIN.

A Romantic Dinner

GRATIN OF BREADED OYSTERS 51

PAN-SEARED OR GRILLED MARINATED FLANK STEAK 112

CARAMELIZED MUSHROOMS WITH SHALLOTS 127

SALAD

RASPBERRY VELVET 156

SPECIAL SEGMENT: DISCUSSION OF GRILLING MEATS

SUGGESTED WINES:
- **BRUT CHAMPAGNE, MUMM CORDON ROUGE**
- **VINO ROSSO RESERVA, SIGLO RIOJA 1985**

The first course in this menu demonstrates a delicious and different way of preparing oysters. They are first blanched in their own juices, then arranged in a gratin dish with seasoned bread crumbs on top, and finished under a hot broiler. I follow this with a flank steak, trimmed of all surrounding fat and marinated in a piquant mixture of honey, soy sauce, garlic, coriander, and cayenne pepper before it is grilled or pan-seared at serving time. While not too many years ago it was thought that a steak weighing 1¼ pounds would feed only one person, my flank steak of that weight is sufficient for four when it is cut on the bias into thin slices. Tender and flavorful, the steak is served with whole caramelized mushrooms. I like to use older, darker mushrooms with somewhat open gills for this dish, finding they acquire the concentrated taste I want when they are cooked a long time. I conclude with a refreshing berry velvet. Made from a puree of raspberries frozen to a slushlike consistency, this dessert is served in stemmed glasses that are rimmed—margarita-style—with lime juice and sugar.

A Midsummer Night's Tête-à-Tête

GAZPACHO WITH BLACK OLIVES 20

GRILLED LAMB CHOPS RIVIERA 96

SALAD

ICE-CREAM PHYLLO NAPOLEONS 169

SPECIAL SEGMENT: WORKING WITH PHYLLO DOUGH

SUGGESTED WINES:
- **FLEUR DE CHAMPAGNE, PERRIER-JOUET 1988**
- **GEVREY-CHAMBERTIN, PIERRE PONNELLE 1990**

For me, gazpacho is the ideal summer menu starter and, served in larger quantities with an earthy country bread, can almost stand as a meal on its own. A liquid salad, it contains a host of vegetables—among them tomatoes, cucumbers, red bell pepper, and red onion—some of which are cut into chunks for serving as a garnish, while the rest are pureed with garlic, bread, and seasonings to create this tasty, colorful soup. Grilled lamb chops are the centerpiece of this menu. I limit the quantity to one per person and prepare them in the style of the south of France, serving them on a bed of spinach with garnishes of eggplant, tomato, and black olives. After a salad, I finish with ice cream layered napoleon-style between squares of crisp, delicate baked phyllo dough.

LEISURELY SUNDAY DINNER

SPAGHETTI SQUASH IN FRESH
TOMATO SAUCE 32

SLOW-COOKED ROAST
OF LAMB 98

FLAGEOLETS IN *MIREPOIX* 118

SALAD

*TARTELETTES AUX FRUITS
PANACHÉS* 176

SPECIAL SEGMENT:
PREPARING *TARTELETTES*

SUGGESTED WINE:
❧ SAINT-EMILION GRAND CRU,
CHÂTEAU LAPELLETRIE 1989

Even though leg of lamb is generally served rare or medium these days, I occasionally like it slow-cooked until well done, as it is in this menu. Trimmed of fat and sinews, the boneless leg is spread with a mixture of garlic, anchovies, and *herbes de Provence,* tightly rolled, and tied for cooking in a Dutch oven. I serve the lamb with a traditional French accompaniment, flageolets, which are long, narrow beans picked while still light green. They are available— dried, primarily—at specialty food stores in the United States. I cook the flageolets with leek, onion, carrot, celery, and herbs in this recipe and stir a little fresh tomato and olive oil into the mixture just before serving. This summer menu begins with spaghetti squash, much lower in calories than spaghetti and quite good served in the same manner. This recipe features strands of baked squash tossed and served in a garlicky fresh tomato sauce. For dessert, ripe apricot and dark plum wedges are arranged on very thin pastry rounds and cooked in a hot oven until the dough is crisp and the fruit juicy and tender.

THE NEW-FASHIONED COOK

INSTANT SMOKED SCALLOPS WITH
ORANGE-AND-ONION SAUCE 58

VEGETABLE BOUQUET ON
FETTUCINE 86

SALAD

GRAPEFRUIT IN NECTAR 148

SPECIAL SEGMENT:
USING A STOVETOP SMOKER

SUGGESTED WINE:
❧ GAVI DI GAVI,
VILLA MERRIGI 1992

I present a quick smoking technique in this menu, heating a few wood chips to impart a light, delicate, smoky flavor to scallops. The scallops are then served as a first course with a wonderfully complementary orange-and-onion sauce. I continue with a vegetable and pasta dish that is decidedly more "vegetable" than "pasta." Light and colorful, it consists of a host of lightly sautéed vegetables—among them broccoli, mushrooms, zucchini, tomatoes, and corn—served with a modest amount of fettucine. A salad follows, and the meal is concluded with a grapefruit dessert. For this dish, I prepare a caramel, flavor it with grapefruit juice, and pour it over grapefruit segments and a julienne of blanched grapefruit peel.

Fresh and Imaginative

PIZZA OF CURED SALMON AND SOUR CREAM 52

GRILLED CHICKEN WITH TARRAGON BUTTER 80

SAUTÉED *HARICOTS VERTS* AND SHALLOTS 117

ARUGULA AND OLIVE SALAD 115

FRESH FRUITS

SPECIAL SEGMENT: TARRAGON OIL AND BUTTER; SHAPING BUTTER

SUGGESTED WINE: SYRAH, *CAMBRIA, TEPUSQUET VINEYARD* 1992

Beginning with an elegant cold pizza, this menu reflects modern—even trendy—cuisine. The crunchy, delicious pizza crust is made ahead from a dough prepared in a food processor and pressed into round shapes for baking. Just before serving, the rounds are layered with sour cream, thinly sliced red onion, cured salmon (my type of instant gravlax), basil leaves, and black olive pieces. The main course consists of grilled chicken, served with either tarragon butter or tarragon-flavored olive oil, both of which impart the flavor of tarragon but don't have the richness of a standard béarnaise sauce. The chicken is served with two classic French side dishes: For the first, *haricots verts*—very thin French green beans—are cooked until tender but still firm and served with sautéed shallots; for the second, arugula, or *roquette*, is combined with croutons and black olive flakes and tossed in a lemon dressing. A bowl of fresh fruits provides the perfect ending.

Light and Tasty Supper

COLD CREAM OF PEA SOUP WITH MINT 19

CRAB RAVIOLI WITH RED PEPPER SAUCE 72

SKILLET SPINACH WITH NUTMEG 135

SALAD

APRICOT *DÉLICE* 149

SPECIAL SEGMENT: DISCUSSION OF WONTON SKINS AND OTHER ASIAN PASTAS

FOR COOKING: SAUTERNES, *CHÂTEAU LAFAURIE-PEYRAGUEY* 1982

SUGGESTED TABLE WINE: PINOT GRIS, *TRIMBACH RESERVE* 1992

This delightful dinner begins with a refreshing, bright green, cold soup made with very thin-skinned frozen or fresh peas and regular or nonfat yogurt. I use wonton wrappers for the crab ravioli main dish, sealing two around a mixture of crabmeat and chopped herbs. Boiled gently in water just before serving, the ravioli are topped with a red pepper sauce. Spinach with nutmeg—a classic pairing in French cooking—serves as a side dish, and we finish with an apricot dessert. Deep orange, full summer apricots (with sticky juice—the best indicator of ripeness) are poached in a sweet wine that is flavored with basil; then the tender fruit is served in the cooking juices with diced kiwi and basil leaves for decoration.

FEAST FROM THE SEA

MUSSELS *MARINIÈRE* 55

MONKFISH ROULADE WITH BITTER BROCCOLI STUFFING 68

STEAMED CAULIFLOWER WITH CHIVES 120

SALAD

CRANBERRY SOUFFLÉS WITH CRANBERRY-RED WINE SAUCE 154

SPECIAL SEGMENT: PREPARING MONKFISH

FOR COOKING:
- **CHABLIS, *DOMAINE DE LA MALADIÈRE 1991***
- **VOUVRAY, *CHÂTEAU DE MONTFORT 1992***
- **BARBARESCO, *BRICCO MALASPINA 1990***

SUGGESTED TABLE WINE:
- **CHARDONNAY, *LOUISVALE 1991***

Drawing heavily from the sea, this meal begins with a classic French bistro dish—mussels cooked and served simply in a savory, wine-flavored broth. A monkfish roulade is the centerpiece of the menu. For this dish, a fillet of firm-fleshed, meaty monkfish is wrapped around a mixture of seasoned *broccoli di rape* and mushrooms, and cooked on top of the stove. The roulade is served in slices with a sauce created from the monkfish cooking juices, to which are added white wine, tomatoes, and tarragon. Steamed cauliflower makes a delicious side dish. Individual cranberry soufflés complete the meal. Lightly sweetened fresh cranberries are cooked until tender, then half the fruit mixture is used as the soufflé base, with the remainder processed with red wine and served as a companion sauce.

SEAFOOD LOVERS' DELIGHT

TIMBALES OF SHRIMP AND SPINACH 60

SALMON IN SAVORY BROTH 66

CELERIAC AND POTATO PUREE 125

SALAD

SOUFFLÉ OF MANGO WITH MANGO SAUCE 162

FOR COOKING:
- **CHARDONNAY, *STE. CLAIRE 1992***

SUGGESTED TABLE WINE:
- **POUILLY-FUMÉ, *DOMAINE DE SAINT-LAURENT-L'ABBAYE 1992***

For a first course with a touch of elegance, sautéed spinach and shrimp are layered in small timbales or molds, and then the compacted mixture is unmolded onto individual plates for serving. The main dish features salmon fillets poached in a fragrant broth containing lemon peel, lemon juice, fennel, leek, and white wine. The salmon is served with a puree of celeriac and potato, one of my family's favorite side dishes, and this is followed by a salad. A mango soufflé provides an exotic finish to the meal. For this dessert, the flesh of two mangoes is pureed; half the puree is combined with beaten egg whites to create the soufflé, and the remainder is flavored with grenadine and Grand Marnier to serve as a sauce for the dish.

A Touch of the Exotic

CURED SALMON ON FENNEL-AND-MUSTARD-SEED SALAD   44

HADDOCK STEAKS IN RICE PAPER WITH SHALLOT-AND-SOY SAUCE   65

GRATIN OF EGGPLANT AND TOMATO   126

SALAD

BLACKBERRIES IN CREAMY HONEY SAUCE   151

SPECIAL SEGMENT: USING RICE PAPER WRAPPERS

SUGGESTED WINE: ROYALE WHITE MERITAGE, KENDALL-JACKSON 1992

Cured salmon is served on a salad of paper-thin slices of seasoned fennel as a first course in this menu. Cut into ½-inch slices, the salmon takes only about an hour to cure and is deliciously complemented by the mustard seed flavoring on the fennel. As a main course, haddock steaks are wrapped in softened rice paper, sautéed, and served with a shallot-soy sauce. An eggplant and tomato gratin is a light, flavorful accompaniment for the haddock. The healthy new twist in this recipe is that the eggplant slices—requiring a lot of oil when sautéed in a skillet on top of the stove—need only a light coating of oil when baked until tender in a single layer on a cookie sheet. The softened slices are then layered with tomatoes in a gratin dish, coated with seasoned bread crumbs, and finished in the oven. After a salad, the meal ends with blackberries served in a smooth honey sauce with a nonfat yogurt base.

The Unconventional Cook

WALNUT SAUSAGE   62

LENTIL AND POTATO SALAD   61

STUFFED ZUCCHINI "BOATS" WITH RED PEPPER-TOMATO SAUCE   78

SALAD

MERINGUE CHOCOLATE MOUSSE   170

FOR COOKING: VALPOLICELLA AMARONE, CAMPANOLA 1988

SUGGESTED TABLE WINE: MOULIN-À-VENT, DOMAINE DIOCHON 1993

This menu, composed of dishes that all can be brought to the table at one time, goes to the core of what we are attempting to do in *Today's Gourmet*. I love sausage but limit my consumption of commercially made varieties, since most of them contain at least 30 percent fat. Here, using very lean pork from the loin, fillet, or well-trimmed shoulder, I create a light homemade sausage that contains no more fat than chicken meat. I pair the sausage with its classic companion, potato salad, my rendition of which contains lentils and is seasoned with herbs. As a main course, I hollow out zucchini halves and stuff the resulting "boats" with a mixture of the reserved zucchini flesh, dried mushrooms, onion, garlic, and seasoned bread crumbs. Topped with cheese, the "boats" are baked, then broiled briefly, and served with a colorful sauce redolent of tomato and red pepper. A fat-free chocolate mousse—made of cocoa powder, espresso coffee, and a boiled-frosting-type meringue containing beaten egg whites—completes the meal.

THE LIGHT SIDE OF CLASSIC CUISINE

GRILLED SWORDFISH WITH SPICY YOGURT SAUCE 49

POACHED TURKEY IN VEGETABLE CONSOMMÉ 90

SALAD

CREAMY RICE PUDDING WITH FRUIT SAUCE 168

FOR COOKING:
❧ ZINFANDEL, KENDALL-JACKSON VINTNER'S RESERVE 1991

SUGGESTED TABLE WINE:
❧ CHARDONNAY, CAMBRIA, KATHERINE'S VINEYARD 1992

This menu exemplifies my philosophy of cooking. I love thick swordfish steaks when they are properly grilled—until just cooked through, so they remain moist. Rather than serve the steaks in the conventional way, however—with melted butter or a high-calorie sauce—I create a piquant sauce with a nonfat yogurt base that replicates the creamy consistency of a rich sauce but has far fewer calories. This is followed by skinless, boneless turkey breast poached and served in a fragrant stock containing carrots, turnip, celery, and dried mushrooms—the latter an especially flavorful addition. We finish with a rice pudding, my version of which contains rice cooked in nonfat milk almost to the puree stage, then served with a fruit sauce.

WINTER FARE WITH A BONUS

SMOKED TROUT WITH SCRAMBLED EGGS ON TOAST 50

STEW OF LIMA BEANS AND MUSSELS WITH SPINACH 74

SALAD

GRATIN OF APPLES, WALNUTS, AND GRANOLA 141

BONUS RECIPE:
COLD MUSSEL AND BEAN SOUP 23

FOR COOKING:
❧ CHARDONNAY, EDMEADES ESTATE 1991

SUGGESTED TABLE WINE:
❧ JURANÇON SEC, DOMAINE BELLEGARDE 1991

An interesting and unusual stew is the main dish of this menu. Dried lima beans and mussels are cooked separately, then the mussels are removed from their shells and served with the beans on soup plates bordered with garlic-flavored spinach. The bonus here is that the reserved bean- and mussel-cooking liquids are combined to create a delicious soup that can be served cold or hot the following day. The smoked trout and scrambled egg dish that begins the menu would also make an ideal brunch main dish. Although, in the classic French manner, the eggs are whisked continuously as they cook, to make them creamy, my mixture is considerably lighter than the standard version, since I use only one egg per person and substitute nonfat plain yogurt for the traditional cream and butter enrichment at the end. I serve the eggs on large croutons with flakes of smoked trout, readily available now in most markets. After a salad, we finish the meal with a simple apple, walnut, and granola gratin. No need to peel the apples for this dish; the cooked peels lend a chewy texture that goes well with the crunchy granola topping.

A Sumptuous Summer Meal

TOMATO AND AVOCADO SALAD 39

SEAFOOD MEDLEY WITH TOASTED BREAD CRUMBS 67

BUTTERED POTATOES WITH PARSLEY 128

SALAD

BROILED FIGS IN PEACH SAUCE 147

SUGGESTED WINE:
CHARDONNAY, *CAMELOT 1993*

We begin this menu with thick slices of ripe summer tomatoes, using them as a base for an avocado salad with a lemon dressing. To continue, a seafood medley—scallops, salmon, and shrimp—is sautéed with shallots, corn, and garlic just before serving and presented with a toasty sprinkling of lemon-flavored bread crumbs. Simple buttered potatoes—extremely good if cooked properly—make the perfect side dish. The secret is to drain the boiled potatoes as soon as they are cooked, return them to the heat momentarily to evaporate any remaining moisture, and serve them immediately, tossed with a little butter, salt, and chopped parsley. We finish our warm weather repast with fresh figs, cut in half and broiled until caramelized on top, then served with a peach sauce.

Hot-Weather Fare

BRAISED SHIITAKE MUSHROOMS ON BITTER SALAD 40

SALMON IN ASPIC WITH HORSERADISH FLAKES 70

SALAD

SUMMER CHERRY PUDDING WITH RUM SAUCE 144

FOR COOKING:
CHARDONNAY, *LA CREMA 1992*
CARDINALE RED MERITAGE, *KENDALL-JACKSON 1989*

SUGGESTED TABLE WINE:
POUILLY FUISSÉ, *PIERRE PONNELLE 1993*

I begin this summer menu with a salad made with bitter greens—radicchio and Belgian endive—although dandelion greens would be good, too, in this recipe. I serve the greens in a garlic dressing with dried shiitake mushrooms cooked in their own flavorful soaking liquid. A classic do-ahead summer dish, salmon in aspic is the light main course of this meal. Salmon fillets are poached briefly in a tasty stock, then molded in a terrine between layers of aspic made from the stock. This mild salmon dish is appealingly accented at the table with pungent flakes of fresh horseradish. After a salad, the meal ends with a cherry pudding. Prepared in the style of English puddings, it consists of puréed fruit layered with pound cake in a bowl. The cake absorbs the juice of the cherries and swells into a compact mass that is then unmolded for serving with a refreshing mango-flavored rum sauce.

COOKING WITH A SPECIAL FRIEND

FOR COOKING:
CHARDONNAY, *LA CREMA* 1992

IN KITCHEN:
VIOGNIER,
***RÉSERVE ST. MARTIN* 1993**

SUGGESTED TABLE WINE:
MERLOT,
***FORTANT DE FRANCE* 1992**

In the part of France where I grew up, near Lyon, a meal commonly begins with a gratin. I create one here with a small amount of pasta and a large variety of vegetables, including eggplant, corn, pattypan squash, tomatoes, and string beans. I specifically select a large, tubular pasta for this dish, because it swells as it cooks, giving me the volume I need with much less pasta (and so, fewer calories) than would be required if a string pasta, such as spaghetti or fettucine, were used. This is followed by my version of a French classic, chicken *chasseur*. Although I season the *chasseur* in the conventional "hunting-style" manner, with onion, tomatoes, garlic, mushrooms, and white wine, I use skinless chicken—a break with tradition that makes my *chasseur* leaner than its namesake. A delightful lima bean puree absorbs the sauce of the chicken well, making it an ideal accompaniment. The perfect ending to this relaxed family meal: a sumptuous white peach tart.

A TASTY POTPOURRI

SPECIAL SEGMENT:
PREPARING A CLASSIC SALAD WITH A YOGURT DRESSING

FOR COOKING:
PORT, *SANDEMAN FOUNDER'S RESERVE*

SUGGESTED TABLE WINE:
ROSÉ DE SYRAH, *RÉSERVE ST. MARTIN* 1993

An amalgam of different styles of cooking, this menu is interesting and flavorful. It begins with a refreshing French summer classic, melon with port wine, which opens the appetite well to a south-of-the-border specialty, chili con carne, served here with plain boiled rice. The conventional chili ingredient ratio—lots of fatty beef to very few, if any, beans—is reversed here. Essentially just flavored with very lean ground beef, my chili features a substantial quantity of red kidney beans along with a host of seasoning ingredients. I follow this hot, spicy dish with crisp romaine lettuce in a refreshing low-fat dressing. The meal concludes with an apple flake confection, consisting of thin slices of apple dried in a convection oven until crisp and served with frozen yogurt.

VEGETABLE ELEGANCE

MUSHROOM-STUFFED WONTONS IN RED WINE SAUCE 34

POTATO AND SPINACH *GALETTE* 76

SALAD

CARAMEL CUPS WITH COFFEE FROZEN YOGURT 172

CRYSTALLIZED MINT LEAVES AND ROSE PETALS 161

SPECIAL SEGMENT: CRYSTALLIZED MINT LEAVES, ROSE PETALS, AND PANSIES

FOR COOKING: ❧ ZINFANDEL, *EDMEADES ESTATE 1990*

SUGGESTED TABLE WINE: ❧ RED BURGUNDY, *FIXIN 1990*

This light menu begins with an elegant pasta dish featuring large wonton wrappers enclosed around a reduction of shallots, leeks, and mushrooms, and served with an assertively flavored red wine sauce. This is followed by one of my family's favorites, a thick pancakelike "sandwich" of potato with a seasoned spinach filling. The caramel cup dessert is a real showstopper. I fill the cups with frozen yogurt and decorate them with crystallized mint leaves and rose petals, a nice do-ahead enhancement for this and other desserts.

GOOD FOODS FROM THE EARTH

CORN POLENTA WITH MUSHROOM RAGOUT 22

GRILLED PORK *PAILLARDS* WITH ROSEMARY 91

POTATO *GAUFRETTES* OR CHIPS 129

SALAD

SPICY APPLE CHARLOTTE 140

SPECIAL SEGMENT: MAKING A CLASSIC VINAIGRETTE

SUGGESTED WINE: ❧ PINOT NOIR, *CAMBRIA, JULIA'S VINEYARD 1992*

What is more "down to earth" than a flavorful corn polenta? Here, I serve this cornmeal dish with a fragrant mushroom ragout or stew as a first course, although it could be served as a meatless main course or as an accompaniment for meat or poultry. Lean pork fillets are butterflied and pounded into thin steaks, or *paillards,* for the menu main course. Seasoned with rosemary, the *paillards* are grilled and served with thin potato wafers (*gaufrettes*) or potato chips, prepared unconventionally in the oven so they don't absorb much fat. We finish with a comforting and always welcome apple charlotte, flavored here with cinnamon, allspice, and cloves.

RUSTIC BREADS AND SOUP

SPECIAL SEGMENT:
SHAPING BREAD LOAVES

SUGGESTED WINE:
MADIRAN,
CHÂTEAU D'AYDIE 1990

In this menu, I particularly want to demonstrate the making of bread—from the big, round farmer bread to the large country bread, which I used to eat as a child. For me, bread is truly the staff of life; it appears on my table at every meal. If properly made, large bread loaves will keep for days, and I make use of some leftover bread here, slicing it for a garnish with cheese atop *garbure* soup, a French meat and vegetable concoction that is a meal in itself. My version of this classic soup—made with well-trimmed pork shoulder—is delicious but much lighter than the original, which often contained poultry, sausages, and other meats. The menu ends with refreshing pineapple and plum slices served in a sauce made of pureed cantaloupe, honey, and a little Grand Marnier.

JOYS OF COOKING

SPECIAL SEGMENT:
GARNISHING ASPARAGUS
EN FÊTE

SUGGESTED WINE:
GEWURZTRAMINER,
STONESTREET 1991

Much of this menu, including the stuffed cabbage main course, can be prepared in advance. The cabbage dish, consisting of cooked cabbage leaves wrapped around a mixture of seasoned barley and a little lean beef, can even be baked ahead in the sweet-sour sauce, then reheated in the sauce at serving time. Asparagus begins the meal. It is served *en fête,* meaning "in a holiday-style," which is a reference to the dish's colorful garnishes of black olives, tomatoes, and capers. For the dessert that completes the menu, packaged wonton squares are poached, then baked until crisp, and filled with bananas flavored with lemon juice, lemon rind, peach preserves, and rum.

Homage to van Gogh

ZUCCHINI AND TOMATO FANS 29

DAUBE OF BEEF *ARLÉSIENNE* 108

SALAD

RED WINE AND CASSIS
STRAWBERRIES 143

FOR COOKING:
~ CHARDONNAY,
*KENDALL-JACKSON VINTNER'S
RESERVE 1993*
~ MOURVEDRE,
STONESTREET 1990

SUGGESTED TABLE WINES:
~ FENDANT DU VALAIS,
GILLIARD 1992
~ CHÂTEAUNEUF-DU-PAPE,
*DOMAINE DU VIEUX
TÉLÉGRAPHE 1991*

Whenever I think of the artist Vincent van Gogh, I am reminded of the south of France and the town he made famous—Arles—which is also the birthplace of the *daube* of beef main dish in this menu. We begin the meal with another favorite Provençal combination, zucchini and tomatoes, arranged here in fan-shaped configurations and baked with herbs until cooked through and brown on top. I continue with the beef and vegetable dish, cooking the meat in a wine-flavored broth that I season and thicken at the end in the authentic *Arlésienne* manner with a powder made from bread, toasted hazelnuts, garlic, and parsley. A green salad makes a great accompaniment for the *daube*. This menu ends with a refreshing fruit dish, this one composed of strawberries flavored with both red wine and black currant or blackberry liqueur.

French-American Fare

SAUTÉED SOFT-SHELL CRABS
ON ASPARAGUS 56

CHICKEN *BALLOTTINE* STUFFED
WITH RED RICE 88

SALAD

PEARS IN GRENADINE 146

SPECIAL SEGMENT:
BONING A WHOLE CHICKEN

FOR COOKING:
~ CABERNET SAUVIGNON,
*KENDALL-JACKSON VINTNER'S
RESERVE 1991*
~ SAUVIGNON BLANC,
FORTANT DE FRANCE 1992

SUGGESTED TABLE WINE:
~ CHARDONNAY,
CAMBRIA RESERVE 1992

This blend of French and American cuisines represents the best of both worlds. I start with soft-shell crabs, a great American delicacy. They are sautéed briefly here and served on lightly cooked asparagus strips with a garnish of tomato flavored with garlic and tarragon. I continue with a classic French chicken *ballottine,* stuffed here unconventionally with a mixture of chewy, red, California-grown wehani rice, dried mushrooms, leek, and chicken stock. The dish is served with a red wine sauce that includes the accumulated drippings from cooking the chicken. The skin of the chicken is left on to protect the meat as it cooks but may be removed after the *ballottine* is sliced, if you want to eliminate a few calories. The meal concludes with Bosc pears cooked in white wine, lime juice, sugar, and grenadine, and served in a syrupy reduction of the cooking liquid.

A Savory Mélange

SQUID AND *POSOLE* HODGEPODGE 54

VEAL CHOPS WITH OLIVE SHAVINGS 99

SAUTÉED LETTUCE PACKAGES 134

FARINA BAVARIAN CREAM CAKE WITH APRICOT SAUCE 166

FOR COOKING:
↝ VINO BLANCO, *SIGLO RIOJA 1991*
↝ PINOT GRIGIO, *BORGO ARMENTI 1992*

SUGGESTED TABLE WINES:
↝ CÔTE DE BEAUNE LES PIERRES BLANCHES, *PIERRE PONNELLE 1992*
↝ MUSCAT DE RIVESALTES, *CHÂTEAU DE JAU 1992*

We begin with an unusual hodgepodge of squid and *posole*. A Native American food made of treated corn kernels that swell to the size of chickpeas when cooked, *posole* has a flavor I find irresistible. It appears frequently in the cooking of the southwestern United States and Mexico, and can be found—dried and canned—in most specialty food stores and some supermarkets. The *posole* is combined with blanched squid, onion, garlic, tomato, white wine, a dash of Tabasco, and tarragon. For our main course, veal chops are sautéed briefly, then transferred to a warm oven while a sauce is made from their pan drippings, onion, a little butter, and shavings of several olive varieties. As a side dish, Boston lettuce heads are cooked, drained, and then folded into neat packages that are sautéed at serving time. We finish with an egg-free pudding. Made with gelatin, a small amount of farina, and a little cream, this light dessert is unmolded for serving with a lemon- and cognac-flavored apricot sauce.

A Chic Townhouse Meal

ARTICHOKES WITH *RAVIGOTE* SAUCE 30

SEARED CALVES' LIVER WITH TARRAGON-LEMON SAUCE 100

RED SWISS CHARD WITH GINGER 133

SALAD

***OEUFS À LA NEIGE* IN PEACH SAUCE 164**

SPECIAL SEGMENT:
MAKING CARAMEL ANGEL HAIR

SUGGESTED WINE:
↝ PINOT NOIR, *LA CREMA 1992*

This elegant winter menu is ideal for entertaining. *Ravigote* sauce replaces the classic accompaniments for artichokes in France, melted butter or hollandaise sauce. *Ravigote,* which means "invigorate," is a much lighter sauce, consisting of wine vinegar, a variety of herbs, capers, and red onion. Seared calves' liver, our main course, is finished with lemon juice, tarragon, and capers for this elegant meal. Cooked at the last moment, it is ideal for a small party. I accompany this with young red Swiss chard, seasoning it here with ginger and jalapeño pepper. The meal concludes with a classic French dessert, *oeufs à la neige,* or "snow eggs," which are conventionally served with a rich custard sauce but are presented here in a delightful, low-calorie, custard cream look-alike, made of peaches pureed with yogurt.

Classic Fall Feast

SPECIAL SEGMENT: PREPARING FRESH RELISH

FOR COOKING:
☙ SEMILLON, LAKEWOOD 1992

SUGGESTED TABLE WINES:
☙ CHÂTEAU BOUSCAUT, PESSAC-LEOGNAN 1991
☙ PINOT NOIR, CAMBRIA RESERVE 1992

The pièce de résistance in this menu is venison steaks served in a sweet-sour sauce. Venison is available now through specialty or fancy food stores throughout the country. It is usually very lean, flavorful, and rich enough so that you don't need large portions. I bought about 1½ pounds of venison for this dish, trimmed it to about 1 pound, and then cut it into individual steaks weighing about 4 ounces each. Lightly marinated in a little canola oil and thyme, the steaks are sautéed quickly and served here, as they are conventionally, with a sweet-sour sauce. Whereas the base of the standard companion sauce is generally a *demi-glace*—a rich brown sauce reduction that restaurants always have on hand—my lighter substitute is essentially made from the venison pan drippings, vinegar, and currant jelly. With the steaks I serve a spicy raw grapefruit and peach relish that also goes particularly well with pâtés, roasts, and even cold cuts. My vegetable side dish consists of sweet potato slices that are boiled and then sautéed in a nonstick skillet until tender and lightly browned. The menu begins with one of my favorites, thick codfish fillets, which tend to break into flakes as they cook. I serve the flakes with onion, tomatoes, and black olives seasoned with tarragon. We finish this feast with slices of ripe mango and pieces of plum that have been marinated in a delightful honey-rum sauce.

GREAT FOOD FOR SPECIAL GUESTS

**SPECIAL SEGMENT:
MAKING YOGURT CHEESE**

**FOR COOKING:
❧ FUMÉ BLANC,
KENDALL-JACKSON VINTNER'S
RESERVE 1993**

**SUGGESTED TABLE WINE:
❧ BAROLO,
BRICCO CASTELLETTO 1989**

This menu is inspired by Italian cuisine, often featured at our house. We begin with an onion and orange salad, ideally featuring long, narrow, red Torpedo onions and blood oranges when either or both are available, along with flat-leaf parsley, plum tomatoes, olive oil, and cider vinegar. I continue with a staple of Italian cuisine, osso buco, which is made with slices of veal shank with the bones attached. The meat is browned lightly and cooked for a long time with seasonings that include onion, leek, carrot, garlic, *herbes de Provence,* and white wine. Finished with grated rind of orange and lemon, the osso buco is served with chewy brown rice flavored with saffron. Consisting of the stigmas of special crocus flowers, this spice is expensive because of the hard work involved in extracting it from the flowers, but it is worth the cost, since only a pinch is needed to season a dish. The meal concludes with a raspberry trifle. Instead of using heavy cream or mascarpone cheese—traditional trifle ingredients—I use homemade yogurt cheese, layering it with rounds of pound cake and fresh raspberries in individual soufflé molds. The trifle is served with a refreshing nectarine sauce flavored with orange juice and cognac.

FIRST
COURSES

COLD CREAM OF PEA SOUP WITH MINT   19

GAZPACHO WITH BLACK OLIVES   20

CORN POLENTA WITH MUSHROOM RAGOUT   22

COLD MUSSEL AND BEAN SOUP   23

ASPARAGUS *EN FÊTE*   24

ZUCCHINI AND TOMATO FANS   29

ARTICHOKES WITH *RAVIGOTE* SAUCE   30

SPAGHETTI SQUASH IN FRESH TOMATO SAUCE   32

MUSHROOM-STUFFED WONTONS IN RED WINE SAUCE   34

GRATIN OF ZITI AND VEGETABLES   36

RED ONION AND ORANGE SALAD   38

TOMATO AND AVOCADO SALAD   39

BRAISED SHIITAKE MUSHROOMS ON BITTER SALAD   40

MELON IN PORT WINE   42

CODFISH FLAKES IN VEGETABLE *BRUNOISE*   43

CURED SALMON ON FENNEL-AND-MUSTARD-SEED
SALAD   44

GRILLED SWORDFISH WITH SPICY YOGURT SAUCE   49

SMOKED TROUT WITH SCRAMBLED EGGS ON TOAST   50

GRATIN OF BREADED OYSTERS   51

PIZZA OF CURED SALMON AND SOUR CREAM   52

SQUID AND *POSOLE* HODGEPODGE   54

MUSSELS *MARINIÈRE*   55

SAUTÉED SOFT-SHELL CRABS ON ASPARAGUS   56

INSTANT SMOKED SCALLOPS WITH ORANGE-AND-ONION
SAUCE   58

TIMBALES OF SHRIMP AND SPINACH   60

LENTIL AND POTATO SALAD   61

WALNUT SAUSAGE   62

COLD CREAM OF PEA SOUP WITH MINT

1 tablespoon virgin olive oil

1 medium onion (about 5 ounces), peeled and thinly sliced (1¼ cups)

3 cups chicken stock, preferably homemade unsalted and defatted (see page 188) or lower-salt canned chicken broth

¾ teaspoon salt (less if canned broth is used)

1 cup (loose) fresh mint leaves

1 package (10 ounces) frozen petite peas, unthawed, or equivalent amount of fresh peas

1½ cups plain yogurt, regular or nonfat

1 tablespoon unsalted butter

1 teaspoon sugar

¼ teaspoon Tabasco hot pepper sauce

This soup is bright green when freshly made. If you are preparing it more than a few hours ahead, do not add the yogurt until just before serving, because the acid in it will tend to discolor the peas, making the soup a darker, less appealing shade. It is important that you use thin-skinned fresh peas or frozen petite peas here for a smooth result.

1. Heat the oil until hot in a large stainless steel saucepan. Add the onion, and sauté for 2 minutes. Stir in the stock and salt, and bring the mixture to a boil over high heat.

2. After reserving a few of the mint leaves to decorate the finished soup, add the remainder along with the peas to the boiling stock. Bring the mixture back to a boil (this will take 3 or 4 minutes), and continue to boil it vigorously over high heat for 3 minutes.

3. Immediately place half the pea mixture in the bowl of a food processor, and process it until very smooth. Transfer the puree to a bowl, and process the remaining pea mixture along with 1 cup of the yogurt and the butter. Strain both batches of the puree through a fine strainer for a smooth soup. (If not strained, the soup will have a slightly granular texture.) Mix in the sugar and Tabasco, cover with plastic wrap, and refrigerate until serving time.

4. At serving time, process the remaining yogurt for a few seconds, until it is liquefied (it should have the consistency of a salad dressing). Divide the soup among four bowls, and swirl 1 to 2 tablespoons of the liquefied yogurt over each serving. Decorate with reserved mint leaves, and serve.

YIELD: 4 SERVINGS

Nutritional analysis per serving:

Calories 200	Fat 10.5 gm.
Protein 9 gm.	Saturated fat 4.3 gm.
Carbohydrates 18 gm.	Cholesterol 19 mg.
Sodium 655 mg.	

Gazpacho with Black Olives

3 ripe tomatoes (about 1 pound)

3 cucumbers (about 1¾ pounds)

1 red bell pepper (about 7 ounces)

1 red onion (about 6 ounces)

3 cloves garlic

3 ounces bread (preferably from a dense sourdough loaf), cut into ½-inch cubes (1¾ cups)

1 tablespoon corn oil

12 to 15 black olives (preferably oil-cured)

1½ cups cold water

1½ teaspoons salt

1 teaspoon paprika

⅛ teaspoon cayenne pepper

2 tablespoons virgin olive oil

2 tablespoons red wine vinegar

This classic Spanish soup is ideal for summer. Low in calories, it is like a raw vegetable salad. The idea is to create a smooth liquid with the vegetables, which is why I push the mixture through a food mill to strain it after it is processed. If you don't object to small pieces of vegetable or tomato skin in your soup, you can serve it unstrained. A little of each vegetable is reserved and diced as a colorful soup garnish along with olive pieces and toasted bread cubes. (See photograph on page 27.)

1. Preheat the oven to 400 degrees.

2. Cut one of the tomatoes in half, and press the halves over a large bowl to remove the seeds and juice. Cut the flesh into ½-inch pieces (you will have about 1 cup), and set them aside for use as a garnish. Cut the two remaining tomatoes into 1-inch pieces, and add them, seeds and all, to the bowl.

3. Peel the cucumbers, halve one of them lengthwise, and scrape it with a spoon to remove the seeds. Add these seeds to the tomatoes in the bowl. Cut the flesh of the seeded cucumber into ½-inch pieces (you will have about 1 cup), and set them aside for garnish. Cut the two remaining cucumbers into 1-inch pieces, and add them to the bowl.

4. Using a vegetable peeler, peel the skin from about half of the red pepper, and then cut the pepper so that you have one peeled half and one unpeeled half. Seed the pepper, and cut the peeled half into ¼-inch pieces (you will have about ½ cup). Set these aside for garnish. Cut the remainder of the pepper into 1-inch pieces, and add them to the bowl.

5. Peel the onion, and finely mince half (½ cup) of it. Place the minced onion in a small strainer and rinse it thoroughly under cold tap water. Drain well, and set aside for garnish. Cut the remainder of the onion coarsely, and add it to the bowl.

6. Peel the garlic cloves, crush them, and add them to the bowl. (You should have about 6 cups of vegetable pieces.)

7. Place the bread cubes in a small bowl, and mix them with the corn oil. Spread the cubes on a cookie sheet, and bake them at 400 degrees for 8 to 10 minutes, until nicely browned. Remove them, and set them aside for garnish.

8. Pit the olives, cut them into ¼-inch pieces (you should have about ¼ cup), and set them aside for garnish.

9. Place the 6 cups of vegetable pieces in the bowl of a food processor. Add the water, salt, paprika, and cayenne, and process until pureed. (If you have a small food processor, do this in two batches.) Then push the mixture through a food mill fitted with a fine screen. Mix in the olive oil and vinegar, and refrigerate the gazpacho until cold. (You will have 5 cups.)

10. At serving time, ladle the gazpacho into four soup bowls, and let guests sprinkle spoonfuls of the reserved garnishes on top.

YIELD: 4 SERVINGS

Nutritional analysis per serving:

Calories 253	Fat 14.4 gm.
Protein 5 gm.	Saturated fat 1.8 gm.
Carbohydrates 29 gm.	Cholesterol 0 mg.
Sodium 1,244 mg.	

Corn Polenta
with Mushroom Ragout

POLENTA

- 2 cups water
- ½ cup yellow cornmeal
- ¼ teaspoon salt
- ¼ teaspoon freshly ground black pepper

MUSHROOM RAGOUT

- 1 tablespoon unsalted butter
- 1 tablespoon peanut oil
- 1 small onion (3 ounces), peeled and chopped (½ cup)
- 5 ounces mushrooms (domestic, wild, or a combination), washed and cut into ½-inch pieces (2 cups)
- 3 cloves garlic, peeled, crushed, and finely chopped (2 teaspoons)
- 4 plum tomatoes (8 ounces), halved, seeded, and cut into ½-inch pieces (1¼ cups)
- 2 small ears sweet corn (8 ounces), husked and kernels cut off (1 cup)
- ½ cup homemade unsalted and defatted chicken stock (see page 188) or lower-salt canned chicken broth

YIELD: 4 SERVINGS

Nutritional analysis per serving:

Calories 187	Fat 7.5 gm.
Protein 5 gm.	Saturated fat 2.5 gm.
Carbohydrates 28 gm.	Cholesterol 8 mg.
Sodium 302 mg.	

This is a satisfying dish that also can be served in larger portions as a meatless main course. Served on soup plates and eaten with soup spoons, it combines soft polenta with a ragout or stew of mushrooms that is particularly delicious when it incorporates some wild mushroom varieties. (See photograph, page 48.)

FOR THE POLENTA

1. Bring the water to a boil in a medium saucepan. Sprinkle the cornmeal on top while you mix it in with a whisk, and stir in the ¼ teaspoon each of salt and pepper. Bring the mixture to a boil, reduce the heat to low, cover with a lid to prevent splattering, and cook gently for 6 to 8 minutes, stirring occasionally, until the polenta is the consistency of a creamy puree. Set aside, covered.

FOR THE MUSHROOM RAGOUT

2. Heat the butter and oil in a large saucepan. When they are hot, add the onion and sauté for 30 seconds. Add the mushrooms, and sauté over high heat for about 2 minutes, until the liquid emerges from them and evaporates. Add the garlic, tomatoes, corn, chicken stock, salt, and pepper, and bring the mixture to a strong boil. Then reduce the heat to medium, and cook for 2 to 3 minutes.

¼ teaspoon salt (less if using
   canned chicken broth)
⅛ teaspoon freshly ground
   black pepper
2 tablespoons chopped fresh
   chives

3. To serve, ladle the polenta into the center of four soup plates, and pour the mushroom stew on top of and around it, dividing the stew among the plates. Sprinkle with the chives, and serve.

COLD MUSSEL AND BEAN SOUP

2 cups liquid from cooking the
   beans for the Stew of
   Lima Beans and Mussels
   (see page 74), cooled
2 cups liquid from cooking the
   mussels for the Stew of Lima
   Beans and Mussels, cooled
½ cup sour cream
3 tablespoons chopped fresh
   chives
¼ teaspoon Tabasco hot pepper
   sauce

YIELD: 4 SERVINGS

Nutritional analysis per serving:
Calories 72	Fat 6.1 gm.
Protein 2 gm.	Saturated fat 3.8 gm.
Carbohydrates 3 gm.	Cholesterol 13 mg.
Sodium 332 mg.	

This is a bonus recipe using the liquid resulting from cooking the Stew of Lima Beans and Mussels with Spinach (see page 74). I serve the soup cold here, but the ingredients can be heated and served hot as well. If you decide not to make this soup when you prepare the stew, freeze the cooking liquid in small plastic containers. Then, when you want to make the soup, defrost the juices slowly under refrigeration for 24 hours before proceeding with the recipe.

1. Place all the ingredients in a large bowl, and mix them together with a whisk until combined. Refrigerate until cool.

2. At serving time, spoon the cold soup into soup bowls, and serve immediately.

ASPARAGUS EN FÊTE

1½ pounds asparagus (about
   20 stalks), peeled and
   trimmed (about 18 ounces,
   peeled and trimmed)
1 cup hot tap water

LEMON-MUSTARD SAUCE
1 tablespoon Dijon-style
   mustard
½ teaspoon salt
¼ teaspoon freshly ground
   black pepper
2 teaspoons lemon juice
4 tablespoons virgin olive oil

24 oil-cured black olives
2 tablespoons drained capers
1 ripe tomato (5 ounces),
   seeded and cut into ½-inch
   pieces (1 cup)
¼ cup (loosely packed) fresh
   flat-leaf parsley leaves

YIELD: 4 SERVINGS

Nutritional analysis per serving:

Calories 209	Fat 19.3 gm.
Protein 5 gm.	Saturated fat 2.5 gm.
Carbohydrates 8 gm.	Cholesterol 0 mg.
Sodium 977 mg.	

En fête means "holiday-style" in French, and I use the term here to underscore the festive appearance of this dish. Cooked, trimmed asparagus spears are split in half lengthwise up to the tip and the stems spread apart and arranged in a "frame" design on the plates. A mixture of colorful olives, capers, and tomatoes is then tossed with the trimmed asparagus stem ends and piled in the center of the "frames." The dish is served with a lemony mustard sauce. (See photograph, page 26.)

1. Place the asparagus in no more than two layers in the bottom of a saucepan, preferably stainless steel. Add the hot tap water, and bring it to a boil over high heat. Cover the pan, and continue to boil the asparagus over high heat for 4 to 5 minutes, until it is tender but still firm. Most of the water will have evaporated.

2. Remove the asparagus from the pan, and spread it out on a platter to speed cooling. When it is cool enough to handle, measure down 5 inches from the tip of each spear, and cut off and reserve the remainder of the stem ends. Then, starting at the bottom of the spears, split the stems in half lengthwise, stopping when you get to the tips and leaving the heads intact. Cut the reserved stem ends into 1-inch pieces.

3. Combine the sauce ingredients in a small bowl.

4. At serving time, mix the 1-inch pieces of asparagus with the olives, capers, and tomato in a bowl. Arrange four asparagus spears on each plate so the tips extend to the edge of the plate and the stalks, spread open where they are cut, connect to create a "frame" around an open area in the center. Arrange some of the tomato-olive mixture in the center of each plate, and spoon some sauce over both the spears and the mixture. Sprinkle with the parsley leaves, and serve.

PIZZA OF CURED SALMON AND SOUR CREAM (SEE PAGE 52).

25

**CLOCKWISE FROM LEFT: ASPARAGUS *EN FÊTE* (SEE PAGE 24);
ARTICHOKES WITH *RAVIGOTE* SAUCE (SEE PAGE 30); ZUCCHINI AND TOMATO FANS (SEE PAGE 29).**

GAZPACHO WITH BLACK OLIVES (SEE PAGE 20).

27

TIMBALES OF SHRIMP AND SPINACH (SEE PAGE 60).

ZUCCHINI AND TOMATO FANS

4 long, narrow plum tomatoes (about 12 ounces)

4 small, firm zucchini, about 1½ inches in diameter and 6 inches long (1¼ pounds)

4 large cloves garlic, peeled

2 tablespoons virgin olive oil

¼ teaspoon salt

¼ teaspoon freshly ground black pepper

½ teaspoon *herbes de Provence* (see page 190)

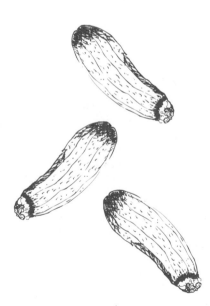

YIELD: 4 SERVINGS

Nutritional analysis per serving:

Calories 104	Fat 7.3 gm.
Protein 3 gm.	Saturated fat 1.0 gm.
Carbohydrates 10 gm.	Cholesterol 0 mg.
Sodium 148 mg.	

This is a great dish in summer, when small, firm zucchini are most plentiful. The idea is first to make zucchini "fans" by cutting the zucchini lengthwise into slices that remain attached at the stem end. Then, with the zucchini fanned out in a roasting pan, long narrow slices of plum tomatoes and thin slices of garlic are inserted between the zucchini slices, and the dish is baked. Leftovers are good served cold with a little vinaigrette on top. (See photograph, page 26.)

1. Preheat the oven to 400 degrees.

2. Wash the tomatoes, and cut each of them lengthwise into four slices. Wash the zucchini and trim off the stem end of each. Then, starting at the flower end, cut each zucchini lengthwise into ¼-inch slices, leaving the slices attached at the stem end so they can be opened like a fan. Each zucchini should have four slits.

3. Arrange the zucchini side by side in a roasting pan or large gratin dish with enough space between so each one can be fanned out. Slide a slice of tomato into each slit and press down firmly on the zucchini to create a fan with alternating segments of zucchini and tomato.

4. Cut each garlic clove lengthwise into eight thin slices, and slide the slices into the fans alongside the tomato slices. Brush the entire surface of the fans with the oil and sprinkle the salt, pepper, and *herbes de Provence* on top.

5. Bake at 400 degrees for 30 minutes, until the vegetables are soft and the fans are nicely browned on top. Using a large spatula, transfer the fans to four plates, and serve immediately.

ARTICHOKES WITH RAVIGOTE SAUCE

2 quarts water

4 firm, dark green artichokes (about 2 pounds)

RAVIGOTE SAUCE

¼ cup coarsely chopped red onion

1 tablespoon drained capers

¼ teaspoon salt

½ teaspoon freshly ground black pepper

2 tablespoons red wine vinegar or sherry vinegar

4 tablespoons virgin olive oil

3 tablespoons chopped fresh herbs (a mixture of parsley, chives, and tarragon), plus 1 tablespoon for garnish

You can cook the artichokes for this dish a day ahead, refrigerate them, then halve them and remove the chokes shortly before serving. A quick reheating in a microwave oven, a regular oven, or boiling water takes the chill off the artichokes, which are best served slightly cool or at room temperature.

The ravigote sauce—a mixture of red onion, capers, vinegar, oil, and herbs—is also good with poached or grilled fish. (See photograph, page 26.)

1. Bring the water to a boil in a large saucepan.

2. Meanwhile, place the artichokes on their sides on a cutting board, and, using a sharp knife, trim about 1½ inches from the top of each. Then, using scissors, trim an additional 1 inch from the tops of all the leaves. Trim the artichoke stems, and peel off their fibrous outer surface. Wash the artichokes thoroughly.

3. Add the artichokes to the boiling water, and place a sieve on top to hold them under the water. Bring the water back to a boil, and boil the artichokes, uncovered, for 25 minutes, or until an outer leaf can be pulled easily from the base and the base of the leaf is tender.

4. Pour the hot water out of the pot, and add enough ice to cover the artichokes and cool them quickly. When they are cool, gently press them between your palms to extract as much water from them as possible without breaking them. Remove the center leaves from each artichoke, pulling them out together in one clump (and reserving the clumps) to expose the chokes. Cut the artichokes in quarters lengthwise and remove and discard the chokes.

FOR THE *RAVIGOTE* SAUCE

5. Combine the onion, capers, salt, pepper, vinegar, olive oil, and 3 tablespoons of herbs in a small bowl.

6. To serve, arrange four artichoke pieces (the equivalent of one whole artichoke) attractively on each of four plates, with the stems extending outward. Arrange a reserved clump of center artichoke leaves in the middle of each plate, and spoon some of the ravigote sauce over the artichoke pieces. Garnish with the 1 tablespoon of herbs, and serve.

YIELD: 4 SERVINGS

Nutritional analysis per serving:

Calories 169	Fat 13.6 gm.
Protein 3 gm.	Saturated fat 1.9 gm.
Carbohydrates 11 gm.	Cholesterol 0 mg.
Sodium 277 mg.	

SPAGHETTI SQUASH IN FRESH TOMATO SAUCE

- 1 spaghetti squash (2½ to 3 pounds)
- 2 teaspoons canola oil
- 2 heads garlic (about 6 ounces total)
- 3 tablespoons virgin olive oil
- 1 onion (about 4 ounces), peeled and chopped (1 cup)
- 3 or 4 ripe tomatoes (1 pound), cut into 2-inch pieces
- 1 teaspoon *herbes de Provence* (see page 190)
- 1½ teaspoons salt
- ¾ teaspoon freshly ground black pepper
- ⅓ cup water
- 1 tablespoon chopped fresh chives
- 2 or 3 tablespoons grated parmesan cheese (optional)

We often enjoy spaghetti squash at our house and occasionally serve it as a low-calorie substitute for pasta. It doesn't taste like pasta, obviously, but its fresh flavor and crisp texture are complemented by pasta sauces. There are different ways of cooking spaghetti squash, but I think roasting it, as we do here, produces a great result and is especially easy.

For the delicious fresh tomato sauce served here with the squash, two heads of garlic are halved crosswise, wrapped in foil, and roasted alongside the squash. Then, when the cloves are soft and nicely browned on their cut edges, their tender flesh is squeezed out and added to a sauce composed of onion, fresh tomato pieces, and seasonings. Mild and tender, roasted garlic can also be served on its own or with other dishes. (See photograph, page 48.)

1. Preheat the oven to 400 degrees.

2. Cut the squash in half crosswise, and scoop out the seeds with a spoon. Brush the cut side of the squash halves with 1 teaspoon of the canola oil, and place them cut side down on a cookie sheet or in a roasting pan.

3. Cut a rectangle of aluminum foil about 6 by 12 inches, and spread the remaining teaspoon of canola oil over half its surface. Cut the heads of garlic in half crosswise, and place them cut side down next to one another on the oiled half of the foil. Fold the unoiled half over the garlic, and fold the edges of the foil together tightly.

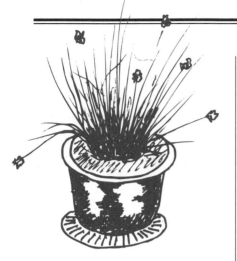

4. Place the foil package containing the garlic next to the squash halves on the cookie sheet or in the roasting pan, and bake at 400 degrees for 40 to 45 minutes. The squash should be tender when pierced with a knife, and its cut sides should be nicely browned; the garlic cloves should be soft throughout, and their cut surfaces should be nicely browned.

5. Heat 2 tablespoons of the olive oil until hot but not smoking in a medium saucepan. Add the onion, and sauté for 2 or 3 minutes. Add the tomatoes, *herbes de Provence,* 1 teaspoon of the salt, and the pepper. Squeeze the soft garlic cloves out of their skins, and add them to the saucepan. Mix well, add the water, and bring the mixture to a strong boil. Cover, and boil over high heat for 10 minutes. Then push the mixture through a food mill set over a saucepan. Set aside.

6. Using a fork, loosen and release the "spaghetti" strands from the squash halves, and mix them gently but thoroughly in a bowl with the remaining ½ teaspoon of salt and 1 tablespoon of olive oil.

7. At serving time, reheat the "spaghetti" until it is hot in a microwave oven for 1½ to 2 minutes, or in a conventional oven set at 400 degrees for 10 to 12 minutes. Reheat the sauce in the saucepan until it is hot, and then ladle a large spoonful of it onto each of four dinner plates. Divide the "spaghetti" among the plates and drizzle about 1 tablespoon of the remaining sauce on top of each serving. Sprinkle with the chives, and serve immediately, with the cheese, if desired.

YIELD: 4 SERVINGS

Nutritional analysis per serving:

Calories 271	Fat 14.2 gm.
Protein 5 gm.	Saturated fat 1.9 gm.
Carbohydrates 35 gm.	Cholesterol 0 mg.
Sodium 878 mg.	

MUSHROOM-STUFFED WONTONS IN RED WINE SAUCE

1 tablespoon peanut oil

1 tablespoon unsalted butter

¼ cup chopped shallots (about 3 large shallots)

⅓ cup chopped leek, half white and half green (about half a small leek, thoroughly washed)

8 ounces mushrooms (all domestic or a mixture of domestic and wild), cleaned and coarsely chopped

½ teaspoon salt

¼ teaspoon freshly ground black pepper

24 wonton wrappers, each 3 inches square (6 ounces total)

I use square wonton wrappers for this recipe. Made of a thinly rolled flour and water dough, the wrappers are especially convenient, since packages are available in the produce sections of most supermarkets nowadays.

The large mushroom ravioli are dropped into boiling water just before serving, and they cook in 4 to 5 minutes. I serve them in a red wine sauce made with a reduction of wine that is flavored with onion, garlic, a little tomato juice, and thyme, but another sauce can be substituted, or the ravioli can be served with just a little melted butter or olive oil drizzled on top.

1. Heat the oil and butter until hot in a saucepan. Add the shallots and leek, and sauté them over medium to high heat for 2 minutes. Add the mushrooms, salt, and pepper, and cook, uncovered, over high heat, for about 7 minutes, until the liquid that emerges from the mushrooms evaporates and the mushrooms begin to brown. Transfer the mixture to a dish, and let cool.

2. Lay twelve of the wonton wrappers out on a flat work surface, and brush them lightly with some water around the edges. Divide the mushroom mixture among the wrappers, mounding approximately 1½ tablespoons in the center of each. Cover with the remaining wrappers, and press gently around the edges with the base of a glass or cup to seal well. Trim the edges, if desired. Arrange the wontons in one layer with no overlap on a tray. Set aside, uncovered (to prevent them from becoming wet and sticky), in the refrigerator until cooking time (no longer than 12 hours).

RED WINE SAUCE

- 1 tablespoon peanut oil
- 1 medium onion (4 ounces), peeled and chopped (1 cup)
- 2 cloves garlic, peeled, crushed, and finely chopped (2 teaspoons)
- ½ teapoon fresh or ¼ teaspoon dried thyme leaves
- 1 cup robust, fruity red wine (anything from a Rhône wine to a cabernet)
- ½ cup tomato juice
- 1 tablespoon soy sauce

- 3 to 4 quarts water
- 1 tablespoon chopped fresh chives

FOR THE RED WINE SAUCE

3. Heat the peanut oil until hot in a skillet. Add the onion, and sauté over medium to high heat for about 2 minutes. Add the garlic and thyme, and sauté for an additional 30 seconds. Stir in the wine, and boil until it is reduced by half. Add the tomato juice and soy sauce, and bring the mixture back to a boil. Boil vigorously over high heat for 30 seconds. Using a blender, food processor, or hand blender, puree the mixture until fairly smooth. Set aside in the skillet. (You will have 1⅓ cups.)

4. At serving time, bring the water to a boil in a large saucepan while reheating the sauce in the skillet. Drop the stuffed wontons into the boiling water, bring the water back to a boil, and boil the wontons very gently for 2 to 3 minutes. Using a skimmer, remove the wontons from the water, draining as much water from them as possible, and arrange them on a serving plate. Top with the sauce, garnish with the chives, and serve immediately.

YIELD: 4 SERVINGS

Nutritional analysis per serving:

Calories 260	Fat 10.6 gm.
Protein 7 gm.	Saturated fat 3.1 gm.
Carbohydrates 36 gm.	Cholesterol 12 mg.
Sodium 894 mg.	

GRATIN OF ZITI AND VEGETABLES

- 2 quarts water
- 4 ounces ziti or penne
- 3 tablespoons virgin olive oil
- 1 onion (about 8 ounces), peeled and coarsely chopped
- 4 ounces string beans, trimmed and cut into ½-inch pieces (1 cup)
- 1 small eggplant (about 8 ounces), cut into ½-inch pieces (2½ cups)
- 1 teaspoon *herbes de Provence* (see page 190)
- 1 pattypan (or another variety) squash (8 ounces), cut into ½-inch pieces (2 cups)
- 1½ teaspoons salt
- ¼ teaspoon freshly ground black pepper
- 2 ripe tomatoes (about 10 ounces), cut into ½-inch pieces (2 cups)
- 2 ears sweet corn (about 1 pound), husked and kernels removed (1½ cups)
- ½ cup black olive shavings, preferably from Nyons olives (about 2 dozen olives)

Only 4 ounces of dried pasta—1 ounce per person—are used in this gratin. Although this is a small amount, remember that ziti, penne, elbow macaroni, and other pastas of that general shape swell dramatically as they cook. Also, since the pasta is mixed with a great many vegetables—onion, string beans, eggplant, squash, tomatoes, corn—the quantity called for is sufficient. The vegetable selection can be altered based on seasonal considerations and market availability.

The ziti and vegetables can be cooked and the dish assembled up to 8 hours in advance, so that at serving time it need only be heated through and browned on top in a hot oven.

1. If you will bake the gratin immediately after it is prepared, preheat the oven to 400 degrees.

2. Bring the water to a boil in a large pot or saucepan. Add the ziti, mix well, and bring the water back to a boil. Boil the ziti, uncovered, for about 12 minutes, or until they are tender yet still somewhat firm to the bite (al dente). Drain and refresh the ziti briefly under cold water to stop the cooking. Cover, and set aside. (You should have 2 cups of cooked pasta.)

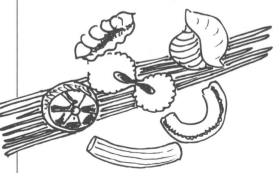

CRUMB TOPPING

- 1 slice fine-textured white bread, processed into crumbs in a food processor (⅔ cup)
- ⅓ cup grated parmesan cheese
- 1 tablespoon virgin olive oil
- ½ cup minced chives

3. Heat the 3 tablespoons of oil in a large skillet. Add the onion and string beans, and cook, covered, over medium heat for about 2 minutes. Add the eggplant and *herbes de Provence,* and cook, covered, over medium heat for 8 minutes, stirring occasionally. Then add the squash, salt, and pepper, and cook, covered, another 2 minutes.

4. Remove the skillet from the heat, and mix in the tomatoes, corn, and olive shavings. Cool the mixture to lukewarm, mix in the cooked pasta, and press the mixture lightly into an 8-cup gratin dish.

5. Mix the topping ingredients well in a small bowl, and sprinkle them over the mixture in the gratin dish. (Note: The dish can be prepared to this point, covered, and refrigerated for up to 8 hours.)

6. Bake the gratin at 400 degrees for 20 to 30 minutes, until it is heated through and nicely browned on top. Serve immediately.

YIELD: 4 SERVINGS

Nutritional analysis per serving:

Calories 415	Fat 19.2 gm.
Protein 12 gm.	Saturated fat 3.6 gm.
Carbohydrates 53 gm.	Cholesterol 6 mg.
Sodium 1,155 mg.	

RED ONION AND ORANGE SALAD

1 red onion, preferably Torpedo (about 6 ounces), peeled

2 seedless oranges (10 to 12 ounces each)

6 ripe plum tomatoes (12 ounces)

½ cup (lightly packed) fresh flat-leaf parsley leaves

CIDER VINEGAR DRESSING

2 tablespoons cider vinegar

3 tablespoons virgin olive oil

1 teaspoon Worcestershire sauce

½ teaspoon freshly ground black pepper

½ teaspoon salt

 This colorful salad is a standard at our house in summer, when tomatoes are at their flavor peak. I like it made with a Torpedo onion, a flavorful, long, narrow, red variety. Although I use regular seedless oranges here to lend acidity to the dish, if you happen to live in an area where blood oranges are available, substitute them instead for color and taste. (See photograph, page 47.)

1. Cut the onion crosswise into ⅛-inch-thick slices. Separate the slices into rings, and place them in a serving bowl large enough to hold the finished salad.

2. Peel the oranges, removing all the white pith surrounding the flesh. Cut the oranges crosswise into ¼-inch slices, and add them to the onion rings in the bowl.

3. Cut the tomatoes in half crosswise, and squeeze them gently to remove the seeds (which can be reserved for stock). Cut the tomato halves into 1-inch pieces, and add them to the oranges and onions. Add the parsley leaves.

FOR THE CIDER VINEGAR DRESSING

4. Mix the vinegar, olive oil, Worcestershire sauce, pepper, and salt in a small bowl.

5. At serving time, add the dressing to the bowl of onions, oranges, and tomatoes, toss the salad, and serve.

YIELD: 4 SERVINGS

Nutritional analysis per serving:

Calories 180	Fat 10.7 gm.
Protein 2 gm.	Saturated fat 1.4 gm.
Carbohydrates 22 gm.	Cholesterol 0 mg.
Sodium 302 mg.	

TOMATO AND AVOCADO SALAD

1   ripe avocado (about 8 ounces)
2   teaspoons lemon juice
1   tablespoon virgin olive oil
¼   teaspoon salt
¼   teaspoon freshly ground
    black pepper
1   large ripe tomato (12 to 16
    ounces)

LEMON DRESSING
1½ tablespoons lemon juice
3   tablespoons virgin olive oil
¼   teaspoon salt
¼   teaspoon freshly ground
    black pepper

4   cups (loose) *mesclun* salad
    greens (a mixture of different
    young, tender greens and
    herbs), rinsed and thoroughly
    dried
¼   cup coarsely chopped fresh
    cilantro

YIELD: 4 SERVINGS

Nutritional analysis per serving:
Calories 220   Fat 20.4 gm.
Protein 2 gm.   Saturated fat 2.9 gm.
Carbohydrates 10 gm. Cholesterol 0 mg.
Sodium 290 mg.

Flesh of a ripe avocado, combined here with a little lemon juice and olive oil, is piled on top of thick tomato slices and presented on a bed of mesclun salad greens that have been tossed with a lemon-flavored dressing. Available now in many supermarkets, mesclun is a mixture of young greens and herbs that are common to the south of France. If you can't find mesclun in your area, substitute Boston lettuce or other greens to your liking.

1. No more than 2 hours before serving the salad, cut the avocado in half, remove the pit, and cut the flesh into ½-inch pieces. In a small bowl, toss the avocado pieces with the 2 teaspoons of lemon juice, 1 tablespoon olive oil, and ⅛ teaspoon each of the salt and pepper. Set aside.

2. At serving time, cut the tomato into four thick slices, and sprinkle with the remaining ⅛ teaspoon each of salt and pepper.

3. Combine the dressing ingredients in a bowl large enough to hold the salad greens. Add the greens, and toss thoroughly.

4. Divide the greens among four salad plates. Place a slice of tomato in the center of each plate of greens, and top with the avocado. Sprinkle with the cilantro, and serve immediately.

BRAISED SHIITAKE MUSHROOMS ON BITTER SALAD

16 dried shiitake mushrooms,
   preferably high-quality,
   imported specimens
3 cups hot water
1 small, tight head radicchio
   (about 5 ounces)
1 large, tight head Belgian
   endive (4 to 5 ounces)

GARLIC DRESSING
1 or 2 cloves garlic, peeled,
   crushed, and finely chopped
   (1 teaspoon)
¼ teaspoon salt
¼ teaspoon freshly ground
   black pepper
4 teaspoons red wine vinegar
3 tablespoons virgin olive oil

¼ teaspoon salt
¼ teaspoon freshly ground
   black pepper
1½ tablespoons virgin olive oil
2 to 3 tablespoons water, as
   needed
12 fresh basil leaves, coarsely
   shredded

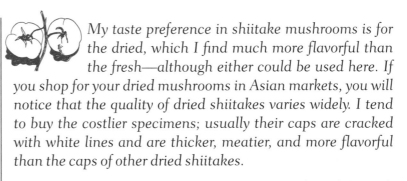

My taste preference in shiitake mushrooms is for the dried, which I find much more flavorful than the fresh—although either could be used here. If you shop for your dried mushrooms in Asian markets, you will notice that the quality of dried shiitakes varies widely. I tend to buy the costlier specimens; usually their caps are cracked with white lines and are thicker, meatier, and more flavorful than the caps of other dried shiitakes.

When soaked in water, the mushrooms create a flavorful liquid; some of this is used here in cooking the mushrooms; reserve the remainder to use later in stocks or soups. Likewise, save the mushroom stems—although too fibrous and tough for this dish, they are good in stocks and, finely chopped, in stuffings.

In combination with the mushrooms, bitter-tasting radicchio and Belgium endive give distinction to this first course. (See photograph, page 47.)

1. Place the mushrooms in a bowl, and cover them with the hot water. Let soak for 1 to 2 hours, stirring them occasionally.

2. Drain the mushrooms (reserving the soaking liquid), and remove the stems. Reserve 1½ cups of the liquid for use in cooking the mushrooms. Cover and refrigerate the remaining liquid and the mushroom stems for use in soups, stocks, or sauces.

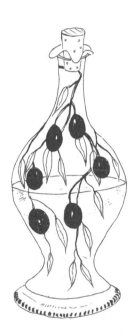

3. No more than 1 hour before serving time, rinse and dry the radicchio and endive heads, if needed. Cut the radicchio in half lengthwise (through the stem) and then into 1-inch pieces; place in a bowl. Cut the endive in half lengthwise and then into ¼-inch-wide lengthwise sticks or strips; place in another bowl.

FOR THE GARLIC DRESSING

4. Combine all the dressing ingredients in a bowl, then divide the dressing between the radicchio and the endive, and toss well.

5. Place the shiitake caps flat in one layer in a large skillet, and add the 1½ cups reserved mushroom-soaking liquid, ¼ teaspoon salt, ¼ teaspoon pepper, and 1½ tablespoons oil. Bring the mixture to a boil, reduce the heat to medium, cover, and boil gently for about 12 minutes, removing the lid occasionally and adding a few tablespoons of water as needed, until the caps are cooked and most of the liquid has evaporated. Uncover, and continue cooking the mushrooms until all the liquid is gone, 3 or 4 minutes. Then cook 3 to 4 minutes longer, turning the caps occasionally, until they are lightly browned on both sides.

6. To serve, make a border of endive around the edge of each of four plates, and pile the radicchio in the center. Sprinkle the shredded basil over the endive and radicchio, and arrange the mushroom caps on top so that about half are cap side up and half gill side up. Serve immediately.

YIELD: 4 SERVINGS

Nutritional analysis per serving:

Calories 180	Fat 15.4 gm.
Protein 2 gm.	Saturated fat 2.1 gm.
Carbohydrates 11 gm.	Cholesterol 0 mg.
Sodium 277 mg.	

MELON IN PORT WINE

1 ripe cantaloupe (2¾ to 3 pounds)
¼ cup good-quality port wine
2 or 4 sprigs sage
Freshly ground black pepper (optional)

This dish is often served in France as a first course. The melon of choice there is the small, flavorful cavaillon—named for the town in the south of France where it was first grown—and one melon is traditionally served per person. I substitute a ripe cantaloupe, which will serve four people, in my rendition of this classic dish. After first scooping as many balls from the fruit as possible, I scrape out the remaining flesh and create a sauce from these trimmings. The melon balls are marinated in this sauce and some port wine, and served, if desired, with a sprinkling of pepper.

1. Cut the cantaloupe in half crosswise. Spoon out and discard the seeds. Using a melon baller, scoop out a layer of balls from the flesh of one of the halves, and place them in a bowl. Then, still using the melon baller, scrape out the flesh trimmings from between the holes, and set them aside in another bowl. Repeat this procedure, working layer by layer, until all the flesh has been removed from both melon halves. You should have about 2½ cups of melon balls and 1 cup of trimmings. Reserve the empty melon shells.

2. Add the port to the bowl containing the melon balls, and mix thoroughly. Place the melon trimmings in the bowl of a food processor or blender, and liquefy them. Add this mixture to the melon balls, mix well, cover, and refrigerate for at least 1 or 2 hours.

3. Meanwhile, using a sharp paring knife, cut the edge of each reserved melon shell into decorative pointed "teeth."

4. At serving time, fill the shells with the melon balls and marinade, and decorate each with a sprig of sage. At the table, spoon the melon balls onto individual dessert plates, and serve cold with freshly ground pepper sprinkled on top, if desired. *Alternative serving method:* Discard the melon shells. Serve the melon balls and marinade in glass goblets, garnishing each with a sprig of sage and several grindings of black pepper, if desired.

YIELD: 4 SERVINGS

Nutritional analysis per serving:

Calories 80	Fat 0.5 gm.
Protein 1 gm.	Saturated fat 0 gm.
Carbohydrates 15 gm.	Cholesterol 0 mg.
Sodium 16 mg.	

Codfish Flakes in Vegetable Brunoise

2 tablespoons peanut oil

1 tablespoon unsalted butter

1 medium onion (6 ounces), peeled and finely chopped (1 cup)

4 pieces codfish fillet, each about 1¼ inches thick (1¼ pounds total)

2 small, firm zucchini (10 ounces), washed and cut into ½-inch dice (2 cups)

1 teaspoon salt

½ teaspoon freshly ground black pepper

⅔ cup dry, fruity white wine

6 plum tomatoes (13 ounces), seeded and cut into ½-inch dice (2 cups)

¼ cup diced black olives (½-inch dice)

2 teaspoons chopped fresh tarragon

I like scrod, haddock, and pollock, but my first preference in this fish family is cod—especially when it is presented, as it is here, in thick, heavy, white fillets. Cod fillets tend to separate into beautiful flakes as they cook, and the idea in this recipe is to combine those natural flakes with sautéed onions, zucchini, tomatoes, and black olives, all of which are scented with tarragon.

1. Heat the oil and butter until they are hot in a large saucepan. Add the onion, and sauté for 1 minute. Add the cod in one layer along with the zucchini, salt, pepper, and wine. Bring the mixture to a boil, cover, reduce the heat, and cook for about 3 minutes, until the fish flakes but is still slightly underdone in the center.

2. Transfer the fish to a platter, and cover it with a pan lid so it stays warm and continues to cook in its own residual heat.

3. Add the tomatoes and olives to the skillet, and sauté them, uncovered, for 1 minute. Add the tarragon, and mix it in.

4. To serve, arrange the codfish, which will flake into pieces, on four dinner plates. Divide the vegetable mixture, juice and all, among the plates, and mix it gently into the fish flakes. Serve immediately.

YIELD: 4 SERVINGS

Nutritional analysis per serving:

Calories 281	Fat 11.9 gm.
Protein 27 gm.	Saturated fat 3.3 gm.
Carbohydrates 10 gm.	Cholesterol 69 mg.
Sodium 14 mg.	

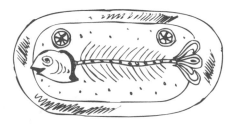

CURED SALMON ON FENNEL-AND-MUSTARD-SEED SALAD

CURED SALMON

- 1 center-cut fillet of salmon about 6 inches square (1 pound total), skin, dark flesh, bones, and sinews removed (about 14 ounces trimmed)
- ¾ teaspoon salt
- ½ teaspoon coarsely ground black pepper
- ½ teaspoon sugar

FENNEL SALAD

- ½ bulb of fennel (about 6 ounces), ribs removed and ½ cup of the fuzzy fennel leaves reserved for garnish
- 1 tablespoon cider vinegar
- 2 teaspoons peanut oil
- 1 teaspoon sesame oil
- ½ teaspoon salt
- ½ teaspoon black mustard seeds

- 1 tablespoon drained capers
- 1 tablespoon virgin olive oil (optional)

YIELD: 4 SERVINGS

Nutritional analysis per serving:

Calories 183	Fat 9.8 gm.
Protein 20 gm.	Saturated fat 1.5 gm.
Carbohydrates 2 gm.	Cholesterol 55 mg.
Sodium 822 mg.	

In this recipe, thin slices of salmon are cured in a mixture of salt, pepper, and sugar, then served on top of a salad made of paper-thin slices of fennel seasoned with black mustard seeds.

FOR THE CURED SALMON

1. Cut the salmon fillet crosswise into 12 slices, each about ½ inch thick.

2. Mix the ¾ teaspoon salt, the pepper, and the sugar in a small bowl. Sprinkle half this mixture on a sheet of plastic wrap large enough to hold the salmon slices. Transfer the slices to the plastic wrap, placing them flat and close together on top of the seasonings. Sprinkle the remaining seasoning mixture on top of the salmon, and cover with another sheet of plastic wrap. Wrap the sides of the plastic wrap tightly around the salmon to enclose it completely, and place it in the refrigerator to cure for 1 hour.

FOR THE FENNEL SALAD

3. Meanwhile, wash the fennel bulb and cut it into very thin slices, preferably using either a food processor fitted with a 1-millimeter slicing blade or a hand slicer. Place the fennel slices in a bowl, and add the vinegar, peanut and sesame oils, ½ teaspoon salt, and mustard seeds. Mix well, cover, and refrigerate.

4. At serving time, arrange the salad in a thin layer on a long, oval platter. Place the cured salmon slices on top, and garnish them with the capers, reserved fennel leaves, and, if desired, a tablespoon of olive oil. Serve three salmon slices per person with some of the salad.

VEGETABLE BOUQUET ON FETTUCINE (SEE PAGE 86).

45

SMOKED TROUT WITH SCRAMBLED EGGS ON TOAST (SEE PAGE 50).

CLOCKWISE FROM TOP: ARUGULA AND OLIVE SALAD (SEE PAGE 115); RED ONION AND ORANGE SALAD (SEE PAGE 38); BRAISED SHIITAKE MUSHROOMS ON BITTER SALAD (SEE PAGE 40).

TOP: CORN POLENTA WITH MUSHROOM RAGOUT (SEE PAGE 22).
BOTTOM: SPAGHETTI SQUASH IN FRESH TOMATO SAUCE (SEE PAGE 32).

GRILLED SWORDFISH WITH SPICY YOGURT SAUCE

4 swordfish steaks (5 to 6 ounces each), preferably center-cut, each about 1 inch thick

½ teaspoon canola oil

1 teaspoon *herbes de Provence* (see page 190)

SPICY YOGURT SAUCE

⅓ cup (loose) fresh coriander leaves

¼ cup (loose) fresh mint leaves

2 cloves garlic, peeled

1 piece ginger, peeled, about the size of the 2 garlic cloves

1 small jalapeño pepper (optional)

½ teaspoon salt

1 cup nonfat plain yogurt

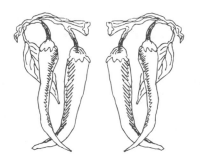

YIELD: 4 SERVINGS

Nutritional analysis per serving:

Calories 251
Protein 38 gm.
Carbohydrates 5 gm.
Sodium 476 mg.

Fat 7.8 gm.
Saturated fat 2.1 gm.
Cholesterol 70 mg.

Thick, white swordfish steaks are a delicacy. Before grilling 1-inch-thick steaks for this recipe, rub them very lightly with oil, and coat them with herbes de Provence, a dried herb mixture that you can find in the spice section of many supermarkets or make yourself (see page 190). Grilling the steaks for 5 minutes marks them and gives them a distinctive taste. Finished in a warm oven, they emerge tender, juicy, and flavorful. The steaks are served here with a piquant yogurt sauce that can also accompany other grilled or poached fish, as well as grilled poultry.

1. Rub the steaks on both sides with the oil, and sprinkle them with the *herbes de Provence*. Arrange the steaks on a plate, cover them with plastic wrap, and refrigerate them until ready to cook. (The recipe can be prepared to this point a few hours ahead.)

FOR THE SPICY YOGURT SAUCE

2. Place all the sauce ingredients except the yogurt in the bowl of a blender or mini-chop, and process until chopped. Add the yogurt, and process until smooth. Set aside, covered.

3. When you are ready to cook the swordfish steaks, preheat a grill until very hot. Preheat the oven to 180 to 200 degrees.

4. Place the steaks on the rack of the grill, and cook them for about 2½ minutes on each side, until well browned. Transfer the steaks to a tray, and place them in the warm oven for 15 or 20 minutes.

5. Spoon enough sauce onto four plates to coat the bottom of each. Place a steak in the center of each plate, and serve immediately. Alternatively, serve the sauce on the side, if you prefer.

SMOKED TROUT WITH SCRAMBLED EGGS ON TOAST

1 smoked trout (about 8 ounces)

4 large eggs

¼ teaspoon salt

¼ teaspoon freshly ground black pepper

2 tablespoons chopped fresh chives

4 slices whole grain or whole wheat bread (about 4 ounces total)

1 tablespoon unsalted butter

2 tablespoons nonfat plain yogurt

YIELD: 4 SERVINGS

Nutritional analysis per serving:

Calories 204	Fat 9.6 gm.
Protein 15 gm.	Saturated fat 3.7 gm.
Carbohydrates 14 gm.	Cholesterol 233 mg.
Sodium 534 mg.	

Scrambled eggs and omelets are commonly served as a first course in France, but rarely so in the United States. I cook the eggs here in the traditional French manner—over low heat while stirring constantly—to achieve the smallest possible curds and creamiest texture, but my ingredients produce a dish much lower in cholesterol and calories than its classic counterpart. For example, I use only one egg per person, and I replace the traditional cream and butter enrichment at the end with nonfat plain yogurt. (See photograph, page 46.)

1. Remove the skin and head of the trout, and separate the fillets from the bones. Break each fillet into pieces or flakes, following the natural lines of the fish. Set aside in a lukewarm place. (The trout should be served at room temperature or slightly tepid.)

2. Using a fork or whisk, beat the eggs in a bowl. Add the salt, pepper, and chives, and beat well. Set aside.

3. At serving time, toast the bread, and trim off the crusts. Place one piece of toast on each of four plates, and arrange the trout flakes around the toast.

4. Heat the butter in a sturdy skillet or saucepan. When it is hot, add the egg mixture. Cook over medium to low heat, mixing continuously with a whisk to create the smallest possible curds. Continue cooking for 1½ to 2 minutes, until the mixture is creamy but still slightly runny.

5. Remove the pan from the heat, and continue mixing. (The eggs will keep cooking because of the residual heat in the pan.) Add the yogurt, and mix well. The mixture still should be moist, soft, and slightly runny. Spoon onto the toast, dividing the eggs among the four plates. Serve immediately.

GRATIN OF BREADED OYSTERS

2 dozen oysters (bluepoints, Chincoteagues, Malpeques, etc.)
1 slice bread
1 tablespoon chopped fresh chives
1½ teaspoons chopped fresh tarragon leaves
2 teaspoons virgin olive oil
½ teaspoon freshly ground black pepper
1 teaspoon oyster sauce
½ teaspoon Chinese chili paste with garlic

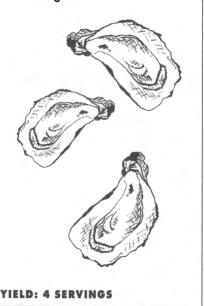

YIELD: 4 SERVINGS

Nutritional analysis per serving:

Calories 100	Fat 4.7 gm.
Protein 7 gm.	Saturated fat 0.9 gm.
Carbohydrates 7 gm.	Cholesterol 47 mg.
Sodium 197 mg.	

This recipe is best made with freshly shucked oysters. Either shuck them yourself, or ask your fishmonger to shuck them at the time of purchase (saving the juice for you in a small container). After the oysters are poached, they are flavored with bottled oyster sauce and chili paste, arranged in individual gratin dishes with seasoned bread crumbs on top, and placed under a hot broiler at the last moment.

1. Rinse the oysters under cold water, and shuck them over a bowl to catch their juices. Place the shucked oysters in a stainless steel saucepan. Allow the oyster juices to sit for a few minutes in the bowl, and then carefully pour them into the pan with the oysters, leaving behind any sandy residue.

2. Bring the oysters and their juice just to a simmer. When the mantles or frills curl on the oysters, set the pan aside off the heat. The oysters will have firmed somewhat at this point but are still slightly undercooked.

3. Break the bread into the bowl of a food processor, and process it into crumbs. (You should have ½ cup of crumbs.) Toss them lightly with the chives, tarragon, oil, and pepper. (The mixture should be fluffy, not gooey or pasty.)

4. Drain the partially cooked oysters (reserving and freezing the juice for use in soups or sauces). Combine the drained oysters in a bowl with the oyster sauce and chili paste.

5. Preheat an oven broiler. Divide the oyster mixture among four small gratin dishes, and sprinkle the seasoned crumbs evenly on top. Arrange the dishes on a tray, and place the tray on the middle rack of the oven, about 10 inches from the heat. Cook for 5 to 6 minutes, until the crumbs are well browned and the oysters are hot. Serve immediately.

PIZZA OF CURED SALMON AND SOUR CREAM

PIZZA DOUGH

- 1 cup warm (not hot) water
- ½ teaspoon honey
- 1 teaspoon granulated yeast
- ¼ teaspoon canola oil
- 2¼ cups (about 12 ounces) all-purpose flour
- ¾ teaspoon salt
- 1 tablespoon virgin olive oil

CURED SALMON

- 1 teaspoon salt
- 1 teaspoon freshly ground black pepper, plus more to taste (optional)
- 1 1-pound salmon fillet, skinned (14 ounces skinned)

- 2 tablespoons cornmeal
- 1 teaspoon virgin olive oil (for moistening your fingers)
- 1 cup sour cream
- 1 red onion (about 7 ounces), peeled and very thinly sliced
- ½ cup (loose) fresh basil leaves
- 8 black olives, pitted and coarsely chopped

Although presented as a first course here, this makes an ideal snack and also can be served with aperitifs at a cocktail party. The pizza dough, made with olive oil, is prepared in a food processor. You can either let the dough rise at room temperature for 2 hours or, for a more flavorful result, let it proof in the refrigerator overnight. After the dough is cooked, it is layered with sour cream, cured salmon (instant gravlax), onion, basil leaves, and black olives. The cured salmon is also good on its own. (See photograph, page 25.)

FOR THE DOUGH

1. Place the warm water and honey in the bowl of a food processor, sprinkle the yeast on top, and let the yeast proof until bubbly, 8 to 10 minutes. Meanwhile, oil the inside of a medium to large bowl with the canola oil, and set it aside.

2. Add the remainder of the dough ingredients to the processor bowl, and process on medium speed for about 30 seconds. The dough will be soft. Transfer it to the oiled bowl, cover it with plastic wrap, and set it aside for about 2 hours at room temperature or, for a more sour, flavorful dough, overnight in the refrigerator. (You will have enough for two 10-inch pizzas.)

FOR THE CURED SALMON

3. Combine the 1 teaspoon salt and 1 teaspoon pepper in a small bowl, then spread half of the mixture out on a large platter. Cut the salmon into about twelve thin slices (about the thickness of sliced smoked salmon), and arrange the slices in one layer on the seasoned platter. Sprinkle the remaining combined salt and pepper on top. Cover with plastic wrap and refrigerate until you are ready to assemble the pizza. (The salmon will be cured (gravlax) and ready to use in about ½ hour but can be refrigerated for up to 48 hours.)

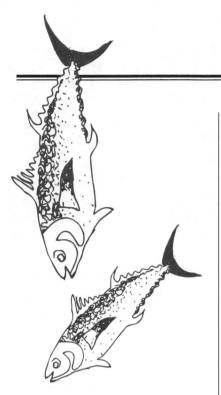

4. When you are ready to cook the pizza dough, preheat the oven to 425 degrees.

5. Break the dough down gently by folding its edges in toward the center and pressing down to release the air. Divide the dough in half, and roll each piece into a ball. Spread half the cornmeal on a cookie sheet, and place one ball of dough on top. Moisten your fingers with a little of the olive oil (to keep them from sticking to the dough), and press the dough into a disk about 10 inches in diameter. Repeat this procedure, shaping the second ball on another cookie sheet. Let the dough disks proof for about 20 minutes, then bake them at 425 degrees for 15 minutes, until they are nicely browned. Remove to a rack, and cool to room temperature.

6. When ready to serve the pizza, spread half the sour cream on the flatter side of each dough disk, and arrange half the onion slices on top. Divide the gravlax between the pizzas, laying the slices side by side over the onions. Top with the basil leaves and black olive pieces, and sprinkle with extra pepper, if desired. Cut each pizza into twelve wedges, and serve.

YIELD: 6 TO 8 SERVINGS

Nutritional analysis per serving:

Calories 383	Fat 14.3 gm.
Protein 18 gm.	Saturated fat 5.3 gm.
Carbohydrates 45 gm.	Cholesterol 46 mg.
Sodium 635 mg.	

SQUID AND POSOLE HODGEPODGE

POSOLE

- 1 can (14½ ounces) yellow or white hominy or ¾ cup dried *posole* (about 4½ ounces)
- 4 cups cold water (if using dried *posole*)
- ¼ teaspoon salt (if using dried *posole*)

SQUID

- 3 cups water
- 1 pound cleaned squid, tentacles left whole and body cut into ½-inch rings (3 cups)
- ¼ cup extra virgin olive oil
- ½ cup chopped onion
- 5 or 6 cloves garlic, peeled, crushed, and chopped (1 tablespoon)
- 1 ripe medium tomato (4 ounces), cut into ½-inch dice (1 cup)
- ¼ cup dry white wine
- 1 teaspoon salt
- ½ teaspoon Tabasco hot pepper sauce
- 1 tablespoon chopped fresh tarragon

YIELD: 4 SERVINGS

Nutritional analysis per serving:

Calories 327	Fat 16.6 gm.
Protein 20 gm.	Saturated fat 2.5 gm.
Carbohydrates 22 gm.	Cholesterol 264 mg.
Sodium 825 mg.	

 This interesting dish can also be served as a main course. Posole, or hominy, is a Native American food consisting of whole kernels of dried corn that have been treated with ashes. The distinctively flavored kernels puff up to about the size of chickpeas (garbanzo beans) as they cook. Although you can buy dried posole in most health food stores and some supermarkets, it requires at least 2½ hours to cook. To simplify and speed the preparation of this stew, you can use cooked canned hominy instead, available in both white and yellow varieties. Squid is a delicious addition here. It is blanched briefly, then added to the stew, and cooked a few minutes longer.

1. If you are using dried *posole,* place the *posole* in a saucepan with the 4 cups of water, and bring the mixture to a boil. Boil for 2 minutes, uncovered, and set off the heat for 1 hour. Add the ¼ teaspoon salt, and bring the mixture to a boil again. Reduce the heat, cover, and boil gently for 2½ hours. Let cool to lukewarm, and drain. If you are using canned hominy, drain the hominy, rinse under cold water, and drain again. (You will have 2 cups.)

2. Bring the 3 cups of water to a boil in a large saucepan. Add the squid, and cook over high heat for about 2 minutes. (The water will not even come back to a boil.) Drain.

3. Heat the oil until hot in a saucepan. Add the onion, and sauté for 2 minutes. Add the garlic and tomato, and mix well. Add the squid, white wine, 1 teaspoon salt, and Tabasco, and cook over high heat for 1 minute, stirring constantly. Add the 2 cups of drained *posole,* mix, and cook for 2 minutes over high heat, until the entire mixture is heated through.

4. Stir in the tarragon, and serve immediately.

Mussels Marinière

4 pounds small to medium
  mussels
1 piece of fennel bulb (about
  4 ounces), cut into ½-inch
  pieces (1 cup)
About 6 scallions (4 ounces),
  cleaned and cut into ½-inch
  pieces (1 cup)
1 medium onion (4 ounces),
  peeled and coarsely chopped
  (1 cup)
4 to 5 large cloves garlic,
  peeled and thinly sliced
  (3 tablespoons)
1 cup dry, fruity white wine
½ teaspoon freshly ground
  black pepper

This is the classic mussels dish you find at bistros in France. Prepared in the style of a marinière, the wife of a marin, a French sailor, the mussels are conventionally cooked with just onion, garlic, herbs, and white wine. My version also includes fennel, which lends a mild anise flavor that complements the other ingredients.

It is important to use small or medium-size mussels that are heavy, indicating plumpness and freshness. Since they are usually grown on lines or nets now, mussels are fairly clean, although you should still rub them against one another under cool water to remove any residual dirt and sand. They cook quickly and are traditionally served as is, with surrounding juices and vegetables. For a fancier presentation, serve the mussels on the half shell.

1. Remove any beards or incrustations from the mussels, and wash them in cool water several times, rubbing them against one another under the water to clean the sand from the shells.

2. Place the mussels, fennel, scallions, onion, garlic, wine, and pepper in a large stainless steel saucepan. Cover the pan, and begin timing the cooking as you bring the mixture to a boil over high heat. Shake the pan occasionally to mix the ingredients, and cook the mussels for 7 to 8 minutes from start to finish. Discard any mussels that have not opened at this point.

3. Divide the mussels, vegetables, and juice among four soup plates, and serve. Or, for a fancier presentation, remove and discard the empty top shells, and serve the mussels on the half shell on soup plates along with the vegetables and cooking juices.

YIELD: 4 SERVINGS

Nutritional analysis per serving:

Calories 188	Fat 3.1 gm.
Protein 17 gm.	Saturated fat 0.6 gm.
Carbohydrates 13 gm.	Cholesterol 37 mg.
Sodium 411 mg.	

SAUTÉED SOFT-SHELL CRABS ON ASPARAGUS

8 asparagus stalks with tight, firm heads (about 6 ounces)

1 large ripe tomato (about 12 ounces)

2 tablespoons unsalted butter

¾ cup chopped red onion

1 teaspoon salt

½ teaspoon freshly ground black pepper

2 tablespoons water

2 tablespoons peanut oil

1 teaspoon finely chopped garlic

1 teaspoon chopped fresh tarragon

4 large soft-shell crabs (about 1½ pounds)

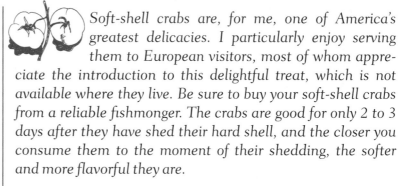

Soft-shell crabs are, for me, one of America's greatest delicacies. I particularly enjoy serving them to European visitors, most of whom appreciate the introduction to this delightful treat, which is not available where they live. Be sure to buy your soft-shell crabs from a reliable fishmonger. The crabs are good for only 2 to 3 days after they have shed their hard shell, and the closer you consume them to the moment of their shedding, the softer and more flavorful they are.

To prepare the crabs for cooking, remove their skirts or aprons, and cut off the strip that includes the eyes and antennae (or have your fishmonger do this for you). The crabs are lightly sautéed here, which makes them tastier and much lower in calories than if deep-fried, which is how they are often prepared in restaurants. I serve them with a mixture of asparagus, tomato, tarragon, and red onion.

1. Peel the lower third of the asparagus stalks, and cut each stalk in half crosswise. (Each half will be about 3 inches long.) Then cut each half lengthwise into four to six strips.

2. Using a sharp vegetable peeler, peel the tomato, cut it in half, and seed it. Cut the tomato flesh into ½-inch pieces. (You should have about 1½ cups.)

3. Heat 1 tablespoon of the butter until hot in a skillet. Add the onion, and sauté for 1 minute over high heat. Add the asparagus, ¾ teaspoon of the salt, ¼ teaspoon of the pepper, and the water. Bring the mixture to a strong boil, and cook it, covered, for 1 minute. (Most of the water will have evaporated at this point.) Transfer to a bowl, and set aside.

4. Heat 1 tablespoon of the oil in the unwashed skillet. When it is hot, add the tomato pieces, the remaining ¼ teaspoon salt, the garlic, and the tarragon. Sauté over high heat for about 45 seconds, just long enough to warm and slightly soften the tomato. Transfer to a bowl, and set aside.

5. Clean the crabs: Lift up the skirt or apron of each crab, and twist or cut it off. Cut off and discard a strip from the front part of the shell that includes the eyes and antennae. Lift up the top shell at both ends to expose the spongelike lungs on either side; pull them off, and discard them. Pat the crabs dry with paper towels.

6. Heat the remaining tablespoon each of butter and oil in the skillet. When they are hot, add the crabs in one layer, and cook them over high heat for about 2 minutes on each side.

7. To serve, divide the asparagus among four plates, and arrange one crab on top of the asparagus in the middle of each plate. Spoon the tomatoes on top of and around the crabs. Pour any juices that may have accumulated in the skillet on top of the crabs. Serve immediately.

YIELD: 4 SERVINGS

Nutritional analysis per serving:

Calories 290	Fat 14.6 gm.
Protein 30 gm.	Saturated fat 5.1 gm.
Carbohydrates 10 gm.	Cholesterol 151 mg.
Sodium 940 mg.	

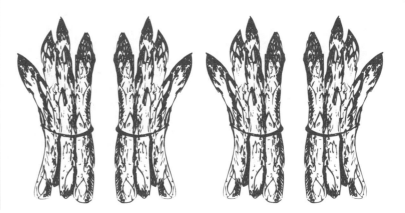

INSTANT SMOKED SCALLOPS WITH ORANGE-AND-ONION SAUCE

ORANGE-AND-ONION SAUCE

- 1 seedless orange
- 1 tomato (about 5 ounces), peeled, seeded, and cut into ½-inch pieces (½ cup)
- 2 tablespoons chopped red onion
- 2 tablespoons chopped fresh cilantro
- 1½ teaspoons red wine vinegar
- 1½ tablespoons virgin olive oil
- ½ teaspoon salt
- ¼ teaspoon freshly ground black pepper

SMOKED SCALLOPS

- 12 large sea scallops (about 1 pound)
- 1 teaspoon corn oil
- ⅓ cup hickory, cherry, or maple wood chips or sawdust

This recipe illustrates a special technique of smoking. The same process can be used to smoke other fish and shellfish. If you do not possess a small commercial smoker that fits on your stove, you can make a smoker from an old pot or roasting pan: Simply place a layer of wood chips or sawdust in the bottom of the pot, and arrange mesh screening so it rests about 1 inch above the wood. Then place the fish or shellfish on top of the screen, and cover the pot or pan with a lid or piece of aluminum foil. When the pan is placed on a hot burner of an electric or gas stove, the chips or sawdust will emit enough smoke to flavor the fish in a few minutes, while generating enough heat in the pan to cook the fish.

Since the amount of wood and the length of cooking time determine the amount of smoke created, you can make adjustments. The scallops here are smoked lightly, as I prefer them, but you can smoke them longer for a heavier taste of smoke, if that is more to your liking.

FOR THE ORANGE-AND-ONION SAUCE

1. Peel the orange down to the flesh, and cut enough of the flesh into ½-inch pieces to make ½ cup. Squeeze enough juice from the remaining flesh to measure 2 tablespoons. Place the orange flesh and juice in a small bowl, and add the remaining sauce ingredients. Mix well, and set aside at room temperature.

FOR THE SMOKED SCALLOPS

2. Wash the scallops under cool water, removing and discarding any white sinews attached to them. Dry the scallops well, and place them in a bowl with the corn oil.

3. Arrange the wood chips or sawdust in the bottom of a smoker, place a screen 1 inch above the chips, and scatter the scallops in one layer over the screen. Cover the smoker, and cook the scallops over high heat for about 1 minute, then reduce the heat to low, and cook 4 minutes longer. (The smoker will be full of smoke, and some of the smoke will escape, but the scallops should not burn.)

4. Set the smoker aside off the heat, and let the scallops cool, still covered, for 10 minutes. Remove the scallops from the smoker. (They will be lightly cooked and have a golden yellow exterior.)

5. Divide the sauce among four plates. Cut the scallops in half and arrange six halves on top of the sauce in the center of each plate. Serve immediately.

YIELD: 4 SERVINGS

Nutritional analysis per serving:

Calories 182	Fat 7.2 gm.
Protein 20 gm.	Saturated fat 0.9 gm.
Carbohydrates 9 gm.	Cholesterol 37 mg.
Sodium 460 mg.	

TIMBALES OF SHRIMP AND SPINACH

10 unshelled shrimp (about
    14 ounces)

¾ pound spinach

2½ tablespoons peanut oil

2 or 3 cloves garlic, peeled,
    crushed, and chopped
    (2 teaspoons)

½ teaspoon salt

½ teaspoon freshly ground
    black pepper

2 plum or pear tomatoes (about
    8 ounces total), peeled,
    seeded, and cut into thin strips
    (julienned)

YIELD: 4 SERVINGS

Nutritional analysis per serving:

Calories 187	Fat 10.2 gm.
Protein 19 gm.	Saturated fat 1.7 gm.
Carbohydrates 6 gm.	Cholesterol 122 mg.
Sodium 446 mg.	

Although this easy dish takes only minutes to pre-pare, it is quite tasty and makes an impressive dinner party opener. If you prefer, you can simply arrange the sautéed spinach on individual plates and spoon the sautéed shrimp on top for serving. For a fancier presentation, I take the dish a step further here, layering the ingredients in small receptacles and then unmolding the compacted mixture onto plates. Tomato strips, sprinkled on top, make an attractive garnish. (See photograph, page 28.)

1. Shell and devein the shrimp, and cut each into three pieces (about 1⅔ cup). Clean the spinach, and discard any large, tough stems.

2. Heat 1½ tablespoons of the oil in a large skillet. When the oil is hot, add the garlic, and sauté it for 10 seconds. Add the spinach, stir well, and add ¼ teaspoon each of the salt and pepper. Cook over high heat for about 2 minutes, stirring occasionally, until the spinach is wilted. Transfer to a bowl.

3. Heat the remaining tablespoon of oil in the skillet. When it is hot, add the shrimp and the remaining salt and pepper. Cook over high heat, shaking the pan occasionally, for about 1 minute, just until the shrimp become firm. Transfer the shrimp to a bowl, and place the tomato strips in the skillet. Sauté for about 10 seconds, just long enough to take the chill off the tomatoes and soften them slightly. Set aside.

4. Line the bottom and sides of four round-bottomed coffee cups or small timbale molds with about half of the spinach, pressing it into place. Divide the shrimp among the cups, and arrange the leftover spinach on top, so that the shrimp are completely covered. Serve immediately (or keep warm for up to 20 minutes in a 200-degree oven). To serve, unmold the timbales onto individual plates, and garnish them with the tomato strips.

LENTIL AND POTATO SALAD

¾ cup dried lentils (about 4½ ounces), preferably imported *lentilles du Puy* (green lentils)

1 teaspoon salt

2¾ cups cold water

4 small to medium potatoes (¾ pound), washed

¾ cup finely chopped onion

3 or 4 cloves garlic, peeled, crushed, and finely chopped (2 teaspoons)

¼ cup chopped fresh herb mixture (parsley, basil, savory, and tarragon)

3 or 4 scallions, finely minced (3 tablespoons)

¼ cup virgin olive oil

2 tablespoons red wine vinegar

½ teaspoon freshly ground black pepper

YIELD: 4 SERVINGS

Nutritional analysis per serving:

Calories 315	Fat 13.9 gm.
Protein 11 gm.	Saturated fat 1.8 gm.
Carbohydrates 39 gm.	Cholesterol 0 mg.
Sodium 562 mg.	

Sausage is a classic accompaniment for potato salad and is often served with lentils, so it seems appropriate to serve this herb-flavored salad containing both vegetables with Walnut Sausage (see page 62). In my salad, I use tiny green lentils, named lentilles du Puy, *after their place of origin in the center of France. Obtainable at specialty food stores and some supermarkets, this variety holds its shape very well as it cooks. You can, however, substitute another dried lentil in this dish if you can't find lentilles du Puy.*

1. Place the lentils and ¼ teaspoon of the salt in a large saucepan with the cold water. Bring to a boil, cover, and boil gently for 45 minutes, until the lentils are tender. Set the pan off the heat, and let the lentils cool for 15 minutes at room temperature. (Most of the liquid should have evaporated.)

2. Meanwhile, place the potatoes in a saucepan with enough cold water to cover them. Bring to a boil over high heat, reduce the heat to low, and cook the potatoes gently, uncovered, for about 35 minutes (replacing water as needed to keep the potatoes covered) or until tender when pierced with the point of a knife. Drain the water, and let the potatoes cool to lukewarm.

3. When the potatoes are cool enough to handle, cut them crosswise into ⅜-inch-thick slices, and place them in a bowl. Add the lentils, and combine them gently with the potatoes. Add the onion, garlic, herbs, scallions, olive oil, vinegar, pepper, and remaining ¾ teaspoon salt, and mix just enough to combine well.

4. Transfer the salad to a large platter. Serve it immediately, while still lukewarm, with ¾-inch-thick slices of Walnut Sausage (see page 62) arranged on top, if desired.

WALNUT SAUSAGE

1 pound very lean pork (chops, shoulder, or fillet), trimmed to remove all fat and sinews

3 tablespoons crushed ice

2 tablespoons dry red wine

2 cloves garlic, peeled, crushed, and chopped

1½ teaspoons salt

½ teaspoon crushed black peppercorns

3 tablespoons walnut pieces

⅛ teaspoon potassium nitrate (saltpeter or pink salt) (optional)

YIELD: 4 SERVINGS

Nutritional analysis per serving:

Calories 203

Protein 26 gm.

Carbohydrates 2 gm.

Sodium 900 mg.

Fat 9.2 gm.

Saturated fat 2.3 gm.

Cholesterol 72 mg.

I am very fond of sausages and especially like this light version served with Lentil and Potato Salad (see page 61). Whereas commercial sausages contain a minimum of 30 percent fat, these are made with very lean pork and a little crushed ice to replace some of the moisture lost with the elimination of most of the fat.

The sausage is flavored with garlic, red wine, and freshly crushed black peppercorns. To crush peppercorns, spread them on a cutting board and press on them with the base of a small, heavy pan, rolling the pan back and forth over them.

I use a small amount of saltpeter, available at drugstores, to preserve the pink color of the pork in these sausages (which will otherwise turn gray), but its use is optional. I advocate refrigerating the sausages to cure for at least 3 days before cooking, although they can cure there for up to a week.

1. Cut about two-thirds of the meat (10 ounces) into ¼-inch pieces, and place them in a bowl. Cut the rest of the meat (6 ounces) into 1-inch pieces, and place them in the bowl of a food processor with the ice. Process for 20 to 30 seconds, until the mixture is emulsified. Add this mixture to the pork pieces in the bowl along with the remainder of the ingredients. Mix well.

2. Using plastic wrap, shape the mixture into a sausage about 8 inches long and 1½ inches thick. Enclose it tightly in the plastic wrap, and then roll it and seal it as tightly as possible in aluminum foil. Refrigerate for 3 days to cure before cooking.

3. When you are ready to cook the sausage, place it, still wrapped, in a saucepan. Cover with cold tap water. Bring the water to a boil (this will take about 15 minutes), cover, reduce the heat to low, and cook the sausage at a simmer (about 190 degrees) for 10 minutes. Remove the pan from the heat, and let the sausage rest in the hot water for at least 10 minutes and as long as 1 hour. Unwrap, cut into 3/4-inch-thick slices, and serve warm, with Lentil and Potato Salad (see page 61).

MAIN COURSES

HADDOCK STEAKS IN RICE PAPER WITH SHALLOT-AND-SOY SAUCE

4 Japanese rice paper disks (each 8½ inches in diameter)
½ teaspoon salt
½ teaspoon freshly ground black pepper
1 teaspoon finely chopped fresh tarragon
4 haddock steaks, each 3 to 4 inches across and 1 inch thick (about 7 ounces each)

SHALLOT-AND-SOY SAUCE
2 large shallots, peeled and finely chopped (3 tablespoons)
2 tablespoons chopped fresh chives
1 large clove garlic, peeled, crushed, and finely chopped (1 teaspoon)
3 tablespoons rice vinegar
4 tablespoons soy sauce
1 teaspoon sugar
¼ teaspoon Tabasco hot pepper sauce

1 tablespoon canola or corn oil

YIELD: 4 SERVINGS

Nutritional analysis per serving:

Calories 205	Fat 4.6 gm.
Protein 34 gm.	Saturated fat 0.5 gm.
Carbohydrates 5 gm.	Cholesterol 100 mg.
Sodium 1,426 mg.	

 I prepare this recipe often at home, because my wife, who enjoys and frequently cooks Asian food herself, always has a supply of transparent rice paper disks on hand. Available at most Asian markets, they soften when dampened with cold water and make ideal edible wrappers. Here, I enclose seasoned haddock steaks in them, then sauté the steaks, and serve them in their lightly browned wrappers with a delightful shallot and soy sauce. (See photograph, page 101.)

1. Brush the rice paper disks generously on both sides with water, and set them aside to soften for about 5 minutes. In a small bowl, mix the salt, pepper, and tarragon, and sprinkle this mixture on both sides of the haddock steaks.

2. Place each of the seasoned steaks in the center of a softened rice paper disk, then fold the paper around the fish to enclose it securely inside. Place the fish packages in a single layer seam side down on a plate, cover, and refrigerate until cooking time. (The fish can be wrapped up to 4 hours ahead.)

3. Mix all the sauce ingredients in a small bowl, cover, and set aside until serving time.

4. At cooking time, heat the canola oil in a nonstick skillet. When the oil is hot, place the haddock packages seam side down in the skillet, and cook them, uncovered, over medium heat for about 2 minutes. Turn, cover, and cook for an additional 2 minutes. Remove the skillet from the heat, and set aside, covered, for 3 to 4 mintues.

5. Serve one package per person, with some of the sauce drizzled over and around the fish packages.

SALMON IN SAVORY BROTH

1½ teaspoons julienned lemon peel

1½ tablespoons lemon juice

About 3 ounces fennel, preferably from the center where it is most tender, washed and cut into ¼-inch pieces (¾ cup)

About 2 ounces leek, both white and light green parts, washed and cut into julienne strips (1 cup loosely packed)

1 small carrot (2 ounces), peeled and cut into julienne strips (1 cup loosely packed)

2 large mushrooms (2 ounces), washed and cut into julienne strips (1 cup loosely packed)

½ cup dry white wine

½ cup water

¾ teaspoon salt

¼ teaspoon freshly ground black pepper

4 pieces salmon fillet (about 6 ounces each), cleaned of bones, skin, and sinew

1 tablespoon unsalted butter

2 tablespoons virgin olive oil

1 tablespoon minced fresh chives

YIELD: 4 SERVINGS

Nutritional analysis per serving:

Calories 326	Fat 18.6 gm.
Protein 29 gm.	Saturated fat 4.1 gm.
Carbohydrates 5 gm.	Cholesterol 84 mg.
Sodium 502 mg.	

In this recipe, salmon fillets are poached in a flavorful broth containing fennel, leek, carrot, mushrooms, wine, lemon juice, and lemon peel. When peeling the lemon, use a vegetable peeler, taking care to remove only the yellow outer surface of the skin, which contains the essential oils. Then pile the strips of peel together, and cut or shred them finely into thin sticks to create a julienne. Follow these same stacking and cutting procedures when preparing the leek, carrot, and mushrooms, all of which are julienned.

The dish is flavored at the end with a little butter and oil, and garnished with a sprinkling of chives.

1. Place the lemon peel, lemon juice, fennel, leek, carrot, mushrooms, wine, water, salt, and pepper in a large saucepan. Bring to a boil over medium to high heat, cover, and cook for 3 minutes.

2. Add the salmon fillets to the saucepan in one layer, and cook them, covered, over medium heat for 3 minutes, until the salmon is cooked but still slightly raw in the center.

3. To serve, lift the salmon pieces one at a time from the saucepan, and arrange a fillet on each of four plates. Using a slotted spoon, lift out the vegetables, and divide them among the plates, arranging them on top of and around the salmon. To the remaining juices in the saucepan add the butter and oil, and bring the mixture to a strong boil. Pour the sauce over the salmon pieces, and sprinkle the chives on top. Serve immediately.

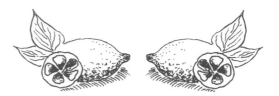

Seafood Medley with Toasted Bread Crumbs

1 piece bread (about 2 ounces), chopped by hand or in a food processor into coarse (1/8-inch) crumbs (1 1/2 cups)

3 tablespoons virgin olive oil

2 tablespoons unsalted butter

8 ounces scallops (12 to 15), washed and sinews removed

8 ounces medium shrimp (12 to 15), peeled and deveined

8 ounces salmon, skinned, boned, and cut into 1-inch pieces (about 12 pieces)

1/3 cup chopped shallots

3/4 teaspoon salt

1/2 teaspoon freshly ground black pepper

4 cloves garlic, peeled, crushed, and chopped (2 teaspoons)

1 ear sweet corn (8 ounces), husked and kernels cut off (1 cup)

1 tablespoon grated lemon rind

2 tablespoons chopped fresh parsley

YIELD: 4 SERVINGS

Nutritional analysis per serving:

Calories 391	Fat 20.9 gm.
Protein 31 gm.	Saturated fat 5.7 gm.
Carbohydrates 20 gm.	Cholesterol 130 mg.
Sodium 687 mg.	

Fast and easy to prepare, this fresh, light dish is perfect for special guests. Scallops, shrimp, and salmon are divided between two very hot skillets and sautéed quickly at the last moment. The use of two skillets is important here, since the fish won't cook properly if crowded into one pan.

The seafood is flavored at the end with corn kernels and garlic, and topped with a mixture of toasted bread crumbs, lemon rind, and parsley, a combination that gives the dish a wonderfully crunchy texture.

1. Preheat the oven to 400 degrees.

2. In a small bowl combine the bread crumbs with 1 tablespoon of the olive oil, rubbing the crumbs gently between your fingers to moisten them lightly with the oil. Spread the crumbs on a cookie sheet, and bake them at 400 degrees for 7 to 8 minutes, stirring them occasionally to brown them on all sides. Set aside.

3. Divide the butter and remaining olive oil between 2 large skillets, and heat until very hot. Then add half the scallops, shrimp, and salmon to each skillet along with the shallots. Sprinkle with the salt and pepper, and sauté over high heat for about 1 minute.

4. Add the garlic and corn kernels, cover, and cook for another 1 to 2 minutes over high heat. Meanwhile, combine the toasted crumbs with the lemon rind and parsley.

5. Divide the seafood among four plates, top with the bread crumb mixture, and serve immediately.

MONKFISH ROULADE WITH BITTER BROCCOLI STUFFING

BITTER BROCCOLI STUFFING

10 ounces bitter broccoli

1½ teaspoons virgin olive oil

2 to 3 cloves garlic, peeled, crushed, and finely chopped (1½ teaspoons)

4 ounces mushrooms, washed and chopped by hand or in a food processor (1½ cups)

¼ teaspoon salt

¼ teaspoon freshly ground black pepper

MONKFISH ROULADE

1 fillet of monkfish (about 1½ pounds), black flesh and sinews removed (about 1 pound, 2 ounces trimmed)

1 tablespoon virgin olive oil

1 tablespoon unsalted butter

¼ teaspoon salt

Monkfish, one of my favorites from the sea, was not really appreciated in the United States until recently. In this recipe, the textured, flavorful flesh of a large monkfish fillet is butterflied, wrapped around a bitter broccoli stuffing to form a roll or roulade, and then cooked on top of the stove. Bitter broccoli (also known as broccoli rabe or broccoli di rape) is a mustard green that appears in Asian and Italian cooking and can be found in most Chinese markets. It is sautéed here with mushrooms and garlic to make a flavorful stuffing for the roulade, which is then served with a complementary tarragon and tomato sauce. (See photograph, page 104.)

FOR THE BITTER BROCCOLI STUFFING

1. Peel the fibrous outer layer of skin from the stems of the bitter broccoli, and cut off and discard the bottoms of the stems if they are tough. Wash the greens well, and cut them into ½-inch pieces.

2. Heat the 1½ teaspoons of oil in a large, heavy skillet. When it is hot, add the garlic, and sauté for 5 seconds, then add the broccoli, still wet from washing, along with the mushrooms and the ¼ teaspoon each of salt and pepper. Mix well, cover, and cook over medium heat for 5 minutes. The broccoli should be tender and the moisture gone from the pan. If any liquid remains, cook the mixture uncovered until the liquid has evaporated. Cool the stuffing to room temperature.

FOR THE MONKFISH ROULADE

3. Meanwhile, butterfly the monkfish to create a ½-inch-thick rectangle about 7 inches by 9 inches. One side of the fillet will be whiter than the other; place the fillet white side down on a clean, flat work surface, and spread the cool stuffing mixture on top. Roll the monkfish to encase the filling,

TARRAGON-TOMATO SAUCE

3 tablespoons dry white wine

Drippings from cooking the
    monkfish (above)

1 or 2 ripe tomatoes (7 ounces
    total), peeled, seeded, and cut
    into ½-inch pieces (1 cup)

¼ teaspoon salt

¼ teaspoon freshly ground
    black pepper

1 tablespoon chopped fresh
    tarragon

and tie it securely with kitchen string. The finished roll or roulade should be about 2½ inches in diameter. Cover and refrigerate the roulade until ready to cook. (It can be prepared up to 24 hours ahead.)

4. At cooking time, heat the tablespoon of oil and the butter in a deep skillet. Sprinkle the roulade with the ¼ teaspoon salt, and brown it on the smooth (unseamed) side over high heat for about 1 minute. Then turn the roulade over, cover the pan, reduce the heat to medium, and cook it for 12 to 15 minutes, or until the fish is tender when pierced with a fork. Transfer the roulade to a platter.

FOR THE TARRAGON-TOMATO SAUCE

5. Add the wine to the drippings in the skillet, and boil the mixture for 1 minute. Add the tomatoes and the ¼ teaspoon each of salt and pepper, and boil for another minute. Stir in the tarragon.

6. To serve the dish, remove the string from the monkfish, and cut the roulade into about eight slices, each ¾ inch thick. Divide the sauce among four hot plates, and arrange two slices of the roulade on top. Serve immediately.

YIELD: 4 SERVINGS

Nutritional analysis per serving:

Calories 213	Fat 10.4 gm.
Protein 22 gm.	Saturated fat 2.5 gm.
Carbohydrates 7 gm.	Cholesterol 40 mg.
Sodium 469 mg.	

SALMON IN ASPIC WITH HORSERADISH FLAKES

1 center-cut piece of salmon
  fillet (1 pound, 6 ounces),
  bones, skin, and dark
  underlying flesh removed
  (1 pound, 2 ounces trimmed)
4 cups water
1 medium onion (6 ounces),
  peeled and sliced (1¼ cups)
½ cup dry, fruity white wine
1 teaspoon *herbes de Provence*
  (see page 190)
1½ teaspoons salt
¼ teaspoon freshly ground
  black pepper
4 ounces mushrooms, washed
  and cut into ½-inch dice
  (2 cups)
½ cup coarsely chopped leek
  greens, washed in a sieve
½ cup (loose) coarsely chopped
  fresh parsley
2 tablespoons coarsely
  chopped fresh tarragon
  leaves and stems
3 tablespoons coarsely
  chopped carrot

This is an ideal summer main course. I poach a fillet of salmon in water flavored with wine, herbes de Provence, mushrooms, and onions, then clarify the poaching liquid, and make an aspic with it while the salmon is cooling. The salmon in aspic is served in slices, with flakes of fresh horseradish root—often available at supermarkets in summer. Its hot flavor goes well with the salmon. (See photograph, page 103.)

1. Cut the salmon in half lengthwise, following the center line of the fillet, to make 2 strips about 3 inches wide and 7 to 8 inches long.

2. Place 3 cups of the water in a 10-inch stainless steel saucepan, add the onion, wine, *herbes de Provence,* 1 teaspoon of the salt, and the pepper, and bring the mixture to a boil. Reduce the heat to low, cover, and boil gently for 5 minutes.

3. Place the salmon strips in the hot liquid (it should barely cover them), and bring back to a light boil. Remove the pan from the heat, cover, and let the salmon sit in the stock for 10 minutes. Then lift out the salmon pieces, place them one on top of the other on a large sheet of plastic wrap, and roll them tightly in the wrap. Cool for at least 2 to 3 hours. Pour the stock through a strainer set over another saucepan, and reserve it. Discard the solids in the strainer.

4. Place the mushrooms in a small saucepan with the remaining cup of water and ½ teaspoon salt. Bring the mixture to a boil, and boil it for 1 minute. Strain through a sieve, adding the liquid to the reserved fish stock and reserving the mushrooms separately. (You will have 3½ cups stock.)

½ teaspoon black peppercorns, crushed with the base of a heavy pan (*mignonnette*)

2 teaspoons soy sauce

1 egg white

3 envelopes (2 tablespoons) plain gelatin

1 piece fresh horseradish root (3 to 4 ounces)

5. Combine the leek greens, parsley, tarragon, carrot, pepper *mignonnette,* soy sauce, egg white, and gelatin in a bowl. Add ½ cup of the reserved stock, and mix well. Set aside.

6. Bring the remaining 3 cups of reserved stock to a boil. Add the leek mixture, and bring back to a full boil, stirring constantly, over high heat. Then reduce the heat to low, and boil the stock very gently for one minute *without disturbing it.* Set it aside to rest off the heat for 10 minutes, then strain it (still not stirring, so the aspic will be crystal clear) through a paper towel–lined strainer into another container. Add the reserved mushrooms to the strained stock, and let cool over ice until the stock is syrupy.

7. Place about 1 cup of the syrupy stock in the bottom of a 6- to 8-cup terrine, and refrigerate until set (about 1 hour). Unwrap the salmon, and pat it dry with paper towels to remove any seeping liquid. Place the salmon on top of the hardened aspic in the terrine, and pour the remaining stock syrup over and around it. (The salmon should be covered.) Refrigerate until the aspic is set, cover with plastic wrap, and refrigerate again until ready to serve. (The salmon will keep, covered and refrigerated, for 2 to 3 days.)

8. Within a few hours of serving, wash and peel the skin from the horseradish root with a sharp knife. Then, using a vegetable peeler, remove small flakes from the root, and arrange in a small serving dish.

9. To serve, cut the salmon crosswise into 1-inch slices with a sharp knife. Arrange a slice on each of four plates, and spoon some aspic alongside. Pass the dish of horseradish flakes. (Note: The flakes are very pungent and peppery; use as desired.)

YIELD: 4 SERVINGS

Nutritional analysis per serving:

Calories 263	Fat 8.5 gm.
Protein 33 gm.	Saturated fat 1.3 gm.
Carbohydrates 13 gm.	Cholesterol 71 mg.
Sodium 1,089 mg.	

CRAB RAVIOLI WITH RED PEPPER SAUCE

CRAB RAVIOLI

- 1 red bell pepper (8 to 10 ounces), halved and seeded
- 1 tablespoon virgin olive oil
- 1/3 cup chopped shallots
- 2 to 3 cloves garlic, peeled, crushed, and chopped (1½ teaspoons)
- 8 ounces cleaned crabmeat
- 1/4 cup chopped fresh herbs (a mixture of parsley, chives, chervil, and tarragon)
- 1/4 teaspoon salt
- 1/4 teaspoon freshly ground black pepper
- 32 wonton wrappers, each 3 inches square (8 ounces total, before trimming)

I stuff packaged wonton wrapper squares with a mixture of crab, shallots, red pepper, and garlic here, then use a round cutter to trim off the dough edges to make ravioli rounds. (I save the trimmings and add them to soups or stocks, as I would pasta.) The ravioli are served with a colorful sauce made with red pepper, onion, and garlic. Thickened lightly, it is finished with a little cream—about 1 tablespoon, or 40 calories, per person.

FOR THE RAVIOLI

1. Peel and chop enough of the red bell pepper to have 2 tablespoons. Reserve the remainder (6 to 7 ounces) for use in the red pepper sauce. Heat the oil in a saucepan until it is hot but not smoking. Add the shallots and chopped red pepper, and sauté for 1 minute. Add the garlic, and mix well. Place the crabmeat in a bowl, and add the mixture from the skillet along with the herbs, salt, and pepper. Mix gently but thoroughly.

2. Lay sixteen of the wonton wrappers out side by side on a flat work surface. Mound approximately 2 tablespoons of the crabmeat mixture in the center of each square. Using a pastry brush, moisten one side of the remaining sixteen wonton wrappers with cold water, and place each (moist side down) in proper alignment on top of a crabmeat-covered wrapper. Press gently around the edges to seal the two wrappers together and enclose the filling. Using a 3-inch-diameter cutter, trim each square into a round shape. (You should have about 2 ounces of dough trimmings, which can be added to soup or discarded.) Arrange the ravioli rounds in a single layer on a tray, cover with plastic wrap, and refrigerate until cooking time. (The recipe can be prepared to this point 6 to 8 hours ahead.)

RED PEPPER SAUCE

- **6** to 7 ounces red bell pepper (reserved from the ravioli), cut into ½-inch pieces, (about 1½ cups)
- **¾** cup thinly sliced onion
- **1** clove garlic, peeled
- **1½** cups water
- **½** teaspoon salt
- **¼** teaspoon freshly ground black pepper
- **1½** teaspoons potato starch dissolved in 1 tablespoon cold water
- **4** tablespoons heavy cream
- **2** quarts water for cooking the ravioli
- **1** tablespoon chopped fresh chives (optional)

FOR THE RED PEPPER SAUCE

3. Combine the red pepper pieces, onion, and garlic with the 1½ cups water in a saucepan. Bring the mixture to a boil, cover, and boil gently for 6 to 8 minutes. Add the salt and pepper, and mix well. Bring to a boil, and boil for 1 minute. Stir in the dissolved potato starch, bring the mixture to a boil, and immediately set it off the heat.

4. Push the mixture through a food mill set over a saucepan. If desired, emulsify the mixture in the saucepan using a hand-held immersible blender, or in a conventional blender, until it liquefies into a puree. Add the cream, and mix well.

5. At serving time, bring the water to a boil in a large pot. Add eight of the ravioli, and boil them gently for 3 minutes. Using a skimmer, lift them from the water, and arrange four on each of two plates. Repeat with the remaining eight ravioli, arranging them on two additional plates. Divide the red pepper sauce among the plates, spooning it over the ravioli. Sprinkle with the chives, if desired, and serve immediately.

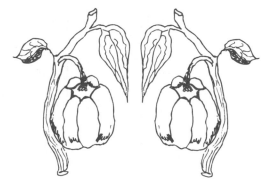

YIELD: 4 SERVINGS

Nutritional analysis per serving:

Calories 307	Fat 10.6 gm.
Protein 17 gm.	Saturated fat 4.1 gm.
Carbohydrates 35 gm.	Cholesterol 81 mg.
Sodium 821 mg.	

Stew of Lima Beans and Mussels with Spinach

8 ounces dried lima beans

4 cups cold water

1½ teaspoons salt

3 pounds mussels

1 cup dry, fruity white wine

4½ tablespoons virgin olive oil

12 scallions, trimmed, washed, and coarsely chopped (1¼ cups)

5 to 6 cloves garlic, peeled, crushed, and chopped (1 tablespoon)

1 pound spinach, tough stems removed and the remainder washed (about 12 ounces, cleaned)

½ teaspoon freshly ground black pepper

 I use large dried lima beans, which cook faster than most other dried beans, for this recipe. As they cook, the skins will separate from some of the beans and rise to the surface; remove and discard the floating skins, but don't attempt to remove the skins from beans that don't shed them on their own.

Mussels are cooked with a little wine and then removed from their shells. Some of the mussel liquid is added to the stew along with the drained beans and mussels, and this mixture is then served with sautéed spinach. (See photograph, page 102.)

As a bonus recipe, the remainder of the juice from cooking the mussels—which years ago would have been transformed into a billi-bi with the addition of heavy cream, tarragon, and chives—is thickened slightly here with the reserved liquid from cooking the beans, a little sour cream, and chives. The result is a flavorful and less caloric soup (see Cold Mussel and Bean Soup on page 23).

1. Wash the lima beans, and discard any damaged beans or pebbles. Place the beans in a saucepan with the cold water. Add 1 teaspoon of the salt, and bring to a boil. Cover, reduce the heat, and boil gently for 30 to 40 minutes, until the beans are tender. (Remove and discard any skins that float to the surface.)

2. Drain the beans, reserving the cooking liquid for use in Cold Mussel and Bean Soup (see page 23). You should have about 2 cups of liquid; if you have less, add water.

3. Rub the mussels against one another in several changes of cold water to remove as much dirt and sand from their shells as possible. Place them with the wine in a stainless steel saucepan, cover, and cook over high heat until they have opened, 7 to 8 minutes from the cold start. Drain, reserving the cooking liquid. You should have 3 cups of liquid; if you have less, add water. Reserve 1 cup of the liquid for use in this recipe, and keep the remaining 2 cups for use in Cold Mussel and Bean Soup.

4. Remove the mussels from their shells, and set them aside in a bowl. If desired, keep a few of the shells for decoration.

5. Heat 3 tablespoons of the olive oil in a saucepan. When it is hot but not smoking, add the scallions, and sauté them over medium heat for 1 minute. Add the reserved cup of mussel liquid, the drained beans, and the mussels. Mix well, and set aside to reheat at serving time.

6. Heat the remaining 1½ tablespoons of oil in a saucepan, and add the garlic. Sauté for 30 seconds, and mix in the spinach. Cover, and cook for 3 to 4 minutes, until the spinach wilts and is tender. Add the remaining ½ teaspoon salt and the pepper, mix well, and transfer any juices that emerge from the spinach to the mussel and bean mixture.

7. Divide the spinach among four soup plates, and arrange it around the periphery to create an attractive border. Heat the mussel mixture until warmed through, and spoon it into the center of the plates. Decorate, if desired, with some of the reserved mussel shells. Serve immediately.

YIELD: 4 SERVINGS

Nutritional analysis per serving:

Calories 433	Fat 18.1 gm.
Protein 26 gm.	Saturated fat 2.6 gm.
Carbohydrates 41 gm.	Cholesterol 28 mg.
Sodium 638 mg.	

POTATO AND SPINACH GALETTE

1   **pound spinach**

1½ **pounds potatoes (3 or 4), preferably Yukon Gold**

3   **tablespoons virgin olive oil**

1   **tablespoon unsalted butter**

½   **teaspoon salt**

4   **large cloves garlic, peeled and very thinly sliced (1½ tablespoons)**

¼   **teaspoon freshly ground black pepper**

This main course vegetable dish is prepared in a non-stick skillet or omelet pan so it will release easily when inverted onto a plate for serving. The word galette *denotes a flattish, disk-shaped pancake here; this one is really a "sandwich" of potatoes panfried in a skillet with a filling of garlic-flavored spinach. This galette is especially good in summer with a green salad accompaniment. (See photograph, page 122.)*

1. If you will bake the *galette* immediately after preparing it, preheat the oven to 400 degrees. Remove and discard the tough stems and damaged leaves of the spinach, and wash the remaining leaves.

2. Wash the potatoes, peel them, and cut them into very thin slices by hand or in a food processor fitted with a slicing disk. Wash the slices, drain them, and pat them dry with paper towels.

3. In a 10-inch nonstick ovenproof skillet (preferably an omelet pan), heat 1 tablespoon of the oil and the butter until they are hot. Add the potato slices, and season them with 1/4 teaspoon of the salt. Sauté over high heat for 2 or 3 minutes, gently stirring the potatoes, until all the slices are coated with oil and butter and are just starting to soften and become transparent. Transfer the potatoes to a plate, and set them aside.

4. In the same skillet (unwashed), heat 1 tablespoon of the remaining oil until it is hot. Add the garlic, and sauté it for 10 seconds. Then add the spinach, the remaining salt, and the pepper, and sauté for about 2 minutes, until the spinach is wilted and most of its liquid has evaporated. Transfer the spinach to a plate, and set it aside.

5. Place the remaining tablespoon of oil in the same skillet, and arrange a layer of potato slices in an attractive pattern to cover the bottom of the pan, extending about ½ inch up the sides. Place another layer of potatoes on top, using half the potatoes for the two layers. Spread the spinach on top of the potatoes, and cover it with the remaining potatoes. (The recipe can be prepared to this point up to 6 hours ahead.)

6. When you are ready to serve the *galette,* bake it in a 400-degree oven for 30 minutes. Remove the skillet, and place it on top of the stove over medium to high heat for 2 to 3 minutes to brown the bottom layer, shaking the pan so the bottom of the *galette* doesn't stick to it. Invert the *galette* onto a large plate or platter, and cut into wedges to serve.

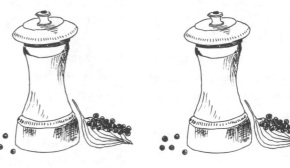

YIELD: 4 SERVINGS

Nutritional analysis per serving:

Calories 263	Fat 13.6 gm.
Protein 6 gm.	Saturated fat 3.2 gm.
Carbohydrates 32 gm.	Cholesterol 8 mg.
Sodium 351 mg.	

Stuffed Zucchini "Boats" with Red Pepper–Tomato Sauce

STUFFED ZUCCHINI "BOATS"

- 6 to 8 dried shiitake mushroom caps (1 ounce)
- 2 cups hot tap water
- 4 small, firm zucchini, each about 2 inches in diameter and 5 inches long (1¼ pounds total)
- 2 tablespoons virgin olive oil
- 1 large onion (8 ounces), peeled and finely chopped (2 cups)
- 5 to 6 cloves garlic, peeled, crushed, and coarsely chopped (1 tablespoon)
- 2 ounces stale bread, preferably from a baguette, processed into crumbs in a food processor (1¼ cups)
- ¼ cup grated parmesan cheese
- 2 tablespoons chopped fresh parsley
- 2 tablespoons chopped fresh chives
- ¾ teaspoon salt
- ½ teaspoon freshly ground black pepper

Although served hot here, this vegetable main dish is good lukewarm in the summer. Stuffed eggplant and zucchini are traditional in both Middle Eastern and southern French cooking. My stuffing includes not only onion, garlic, and bread but also the insides or flesh of the zucchini. The "boats" are served with a colorful sauce made of red bell pepper and tomato.

FOR THE STUFFED ZUCCHINI "BOATS"

1. Place the mushrooms caps in a bowl, cover them with the water, and set them aside for at least 30 minutes.

2. Preheat the oven to 350 degrees.

3. Wash the zucchini, trim the stem ends, and split the zucchini in half lengthwise. Using a melon baller or a metal measuring teaspoon, remove and reserve the seeds and flesh, leaving eight oblong "boats" of zucchini with bases and sides about ¼ inch thick. You should have about 12 ounces (2½ cups) of flesh and seeds; chop this mixture coarsely, and set it aside.

4. Remove the muchroom caps from the soaking liquid (reserving the liquid), press them lightly to remove excess liquid, and chop them coarsely. (You should have about ½ cup chopped mushrooms.)

5. Heat the 2 tablespoons of oil in a large skillet. When it is hot, add the onion and mushrooms. Slowly pour in the reserved mushroom-soaking liquid, leaving behind and discarding any sandy residue from the bottom of the bowl. Bring the mixture to a boil, cover, and boil for 6 to 8 minutes, or until all the liquid has evaporated. Then uncover and cook for

RED PEPPER-TOMATO SAUCE

- 1 ripe tomato (about 8 ounces)
- 1 red bell pepper (about 8 ounces)
- ¼ cup water
- 1 tablespoon virgin olive oil
- ¼ teaspoon salt
- ¼ teaspoon freshly ground black pepper

YIELD: 4 SERVINGS

Nutritional analysis per serving:
Calories 242
Protein 7 gm.
Carbohydrates 28 gm.
Sodium 744 mg.
Fat 12.7 gm.
Saturated fat 2.5 gm.
Cholesterol 4 mg.

another 2 to 3 minutes to brown the onion and mushrooms lightly.

6. Add the reserved zucchini flesh and garlic, and cook, covered, for 3 to 4 minutes, until soft. Transfer the mixture to a bowl, and let it cool to room temperature.

7. When the zucchini mixture is cool, add the bread crumbs, 3 tablespoons of the cheese, the parsley, chives, ½ teaspoon of the salt, and the pepper. Toss the mixture gently but thoroughly.

8. Sprinkle the remaining ¼ teaspoon of salt on the zucchini boats, and stuff them with the mixture, dividing it evenly and packing it firmly but lightly in place. Sprinkle the remaining tablespoon of cheese on top of the boats, and arrange them on a baking tray. Bake at 350 degrees for 30 minutes, then place under a hot broiler for 2 to 3 minutes to brown the tops lightly.

FOR THE RED PEPPER-TOMATO SAUCE

9. While the boats are baking, cut the tomato into chunks, and place it in the bowl of a food processor. Seed the red pepper, cut it into chunks, and add it to the food processor bowl with the water, oil, salt, and pepper. Process until the mixture is liquefied, and then transfer it to a small saucepan. (You will have 2 cups.)

10. Bring the mixture to a boil, reduce the heat to low, and simmer gently for 5 to 8 minutes. Use as is or, for a smoother sauce, emulsify the mixture further with a hand-held blender.

11. To serve, place two zucchini boats on each plate, and surround them with the tomato–red pepper sauce. Serve immediately.

GRILLED CHICKEN WITH TARRAGON BUTTER

1 chicken (about 3 pounds), quartered, with the carcass bones removed (and reserved for stock, if desired)

½ teaspoon salt

TARRAGON BUTTER

1½ tablespoons unsalted butter

1½ tablespoons virgin olive oil

2 tablespoons chopped fresh tarragon

¼ teaspoon salt

YIELD: 4 SERVINGS

Nutritional analysis per serving with skin:

Calories 443	Fat 29.8 gm.
Protein 41 gm.	Saturated fat 9.0 gm.
Carbohydrates 0.3 gm.	Cholesterol 144 mg.
Sodium 532 mg.	

Nutritional analysis per serving without skin:

Calories 316	Fat 18.4 gm.
Protein 35 gm.	Saturated fat 5.8 gm.
Carbohydrates 0.3 gm.	Cholesterol 120 mg.
Sodium 514 mg.	

I created this dish on my stovetop gas grill, but it could also be grilled outdoors on a freestanding gas or charcoal grill. The chicken is grilled long enough so that a great deal of the fat in the skin drains away, and the chicken takes on the characteristics of grilled meat; then it is transferred to a warm oven, where it finishes cooking in its own juices. The dish is less caloric if you remove and discard the chicken skin, but don't do this until just before serving, since the skin keeps the meat moist as it cooks.

A delicious tarragon butter, dotted on the chicken at serving time, replicates the flavor but not the calories of a béarnaise sauce. As an alternative, substitute Tarragon Oil (see page 189) for the tarragon butter mixture, painting it on the chicken pieces with a pastry brush just before serving. (See photograph, page 83.)

1. Preheat a grill.

2. Sprinkle the chicken pieces with the salt, and place them on the rack when the grill is medium to hot. Grill for about 20 minutes, turning the pieces occasionally, until they are nicely browned on all sides. While they are cooking, preheat the oven to 225 degrees.

FOR THE TARRAGON BUTTER

3. Meanwhile, place all the tarragon butter ingredients in the bowl of a blender or food processor, and process until smooth. Set aside.

4. When the chicken pieces are browned, transfer them to a tray, and bake them at 225 degrees, uncovered, for at least 20 minutes and as long as 1½ hours to finish cooking and "relax."

5. Remove the skin, if desired, and serve one quarter per person, dotted with the tarragon butter.

TOP: POTATO *GAUFRETTES* (SEE PAGE 129). BOTTOM: GRILLED LAMB CHOPS RIVIERA (SEE PAGE 96).

PAN-SEARED OR GRILLED MARINATED FLANK STEAK (SEE PAGE 112), CARAMELIZED MUSHROOMS WITH SHALLOTS (SEE PAGE 127), AND SAUTÉED LETTUCE PACKAGES (SEE PAGE 134).

**GRILLED CHICKEN WITH TARRAGON BUTTER (SEE PAGE 80)
AND SAUTÉED *HARICOTS VERTS* AND SHALLOTS (SEE PAGE 117).**

TOP: RAW RELISH OF GRAPEFRUIT AND PEACH (SEE PAGE 136). BOTTOM: VENISON STEAKS IN SWEET-SOUR SAUCE (SEE PAGE 110) WITH SKILLET SWEET POTATOES (SEE PAGE 130).

CHICKEN CHASSEUR

1 tablespoon virgin olive oil

8 skinless chicken thighs, with all surrounding fat removed (about 2 pounds)

1 small leek (5 ounces), trimmed, cleaned, and coarsely chopped (1¾ cups)

1 medium onion (4 ounces), peeled and chopped (1 cup)

1½ tablespoons all-purpose flour

1 cup dry white wine

1 can (15 ounces) whole peeled tomatoes in juice

5 cloves garlic, peeled, crushed, and finely chopped (1 tablespoon)

20 medium mushrooms (about 12 ounces)

1 teaspoon chopped fresh thyme

1 teaspoon chopped fresh rosemary

1 teaspoon salt

½ teaspoon freshly ground black pepper

1 tablespoon soy sauce

1 tablespoon chopped fresh tarragon

 In the original versions of this dish, unskinned chicken pieces were browned in a great amount of butter. Although the skin was crisp initially from the browning, it would soften and become gummy by the time the other ingredients were added and the dish cooked as a stew.

I use skinless chicken thighs in my flavorful update of this dish. After sautéeing the thighs in a little olive oil, I finish them in a chasseur sauce containing onions and leeks and flavored in the traditional manner with white wine, tomatoes, and mushrooms.

This dish can be prepared up to a day ahead; if you do so, however, cook it initially for 15 minutes instead of 25. The chicken will continue to cook a little in the hot sauce as it cools and again as the dish is reheated later, so it will be cooked properly by serving time. (See photograph, page 122.)

1. Heat the olive oil until it is hot in a large nonstick skillet. Add the chicken thighs in one layer, and cook them for 5 minutes on each side over medium to high heat. Transfer the thighs to a large, sturdy saucepan, arranging them side by side in a single layer in the pan.

2. To the drippings in the skillet add the leek and onion, and sauté for 30 seconds. Add the flour, mix it in well, and cook for about 30 seconds. Then mix in the wine and tomatoes. Bring the mixture to a boil over medium heat, and pour it into the saucepan containing the chicken. Stir in the garlic, mushrooms, thyme, rosemary, salt, pepper, and soy sauce.

3. Bring the mixture to a boil over high heat, stirring occasionally to prevent the chicken from scorching, then cover the pan, reduce the heat to low, and cook for 25 minutes. Sprinkle on the tarragon, and mix it in.

4. Serve two thighs per person with some of the vegetables and surrounding liquid.

YIELD: 4 SERVINGS

Nutritional analysis per serving:

Calories 330	Fat 10.7 gm.
Protein 37 gm.	Saturated fat 2.2 gm.
Carbohydrates 22 gm.	Cholesterol 138 mg.
Sodium 1,140 mg.	

VEGETABLE BOUQUET ON FETTUCINE

4 tablespoons virgin olive oil

1 tablespoon unsalted butter

½ cup water, plus 4 quarts for cooking the pasta

About 6 scallions, trimmed, washed, and cut into ½-inch pieces (1¼ cups)

About 6 ounces broccoli, stems peeled and both stems and florets cut into 1-inch pieces (2 cups)

4 mushrooms (4 ounces), washed and cut into ½-inch pieces (1¾ cups)

1 small zucchini (4 ounces), washed and cut into ½-inch pieces (1 cup)

Although I use fettucine in this recipe, any pasta of that general shape—from linguine to spaghetti— would be good served this way. The pasta is cooked at the last moment, then tossed with a puree of garlic, basil, tarragon, and a little of the pasta-cooking water. Finally, it is served with a large assortment of sautéed vegetables. Beautiful and fresh-tasting, it makes a wonderful light entrée for summer. (See photograph, page 45.)

1. Place 1 tablespoon of the olive oil, the butter, and the ½ cup water in a skillet. Bring the mixture to a boil over high heat. Add the scallions and broccoli, bring the mixture back to a boil, and cook over high heat for 3 minutes. Add the mushrooms and zucchini, and cook over high heat for another 2 minutes. Add the corn, tomatoes, ¾ teaspoon of the salt, and ¼ teaspoon of the pepper, and toss the mixture over high heat for about 30 seconds. Set aside.

2. Place the garlic and remaining ½ teaspoon of salt in a mortar, and crush with a pestle until partially pureed. Add the basil and tarragon leaves, and continue pounding with the pestle until you have a coarse puree. Add the remaining 3 tablespoons of oil and ¼ teaspoon of pepper, and continue stirring and pounding the mixture with the pestle until it is smooth. (Alternatively, this step can be done in a food processor.)

3. At serving time, bring the 4 quarts of water to a boil in a large pot. Add the fettucine, and stir well to separate the strands and prevent them from sticking. Bring the water back to a boil, and boil over high heat until the fettucine is done to your liking (about 10 to 12 minutes).

1 ear sweet corn, husked and kernels cut from the cob (¾ cup)

2 plum tomatoes (6 ounces), washed and cut into ½-inch pieces (1 cup)

1¼ teaspoons salt

½ teaspoon freshly ground black pepper

5 cloves garlic, peeled and crushed

1 cup lightly packed fresh basil leaves

2 tablespoons lightly packed fresh tarragon leaves

¾ pound dried fettucine or other flat noodles

Grated parmesan cheese to taste

4. Meanwhile, place the herb puree in a large bowl, and mix in 1 cup of the pasta-cooking liquid. Drain the pasta, add it to the bowl, and toss well. Reheat the reserved vegetables, if necessary, and spoon 2 tablespoons of the vegetable mixture into the center of each of four dinner plates. Divide the pasta among the plates, arranging it on top of the vegetables, and sprinkle the remainder of the vegetables on top. Serve immediately, passing the grated cheese for use as a garnish, if desired.

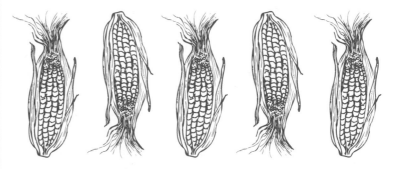

YIELD: 4 SERVINGS

Nutritional analysis per serving:

Calories 557	Fat 21.0 gm.
Protein 17 gm.	Saturated fat 4.4 gm.
Carbohydrates 80 gm.	Cholesterol 89 mg.
Sodium 732 mg.	

CHICKEN *BALLOTTINE* STUFFED WITH RED RICE

RED RICE STUFFING

- ½ cup long-grain red wehani rice
- 1¼ cups homemade unsalted and defatted chicken stock, (see page 188) or lower-salt canned chicken broth
- ¼ teaspoon salt (less if using canned broth)
- ½ ounce dried mushrooms, broken into pieces
- About ½ leek (3 ounces), trimmed, washed, and sliced (1 cup)
- 1 onion (4 ounces), peeled and chopped (¾ cup)
- 1½ teaspoons virgin olive oil
- ¼ cup water

CHICKEN *BALLOTTINE*

- 1 chicken (about 3¾ pounds), defatted and boned, with bones and giblets reserved for other uses (2¼ pounds boned)
- ¼ teaspoon salt
- ¼ teaspoon freshly ground black pepper

A ballottine is a whole chicken that has been boned and stuffed. This version is good family fare and also showy enough to serve company. It can be prepared up to 1 day ahead. Freeze the bones and gizzard for later use in soup or stock. When chicken is roasted at a high temperature, as here, the fat drips to the bottom of the pan and can be discarded. This dish is best cooked in a sturdy aluminum roasting pan, which assures a good crystallization of the cooking juices, used to create a sauce.

The long-grain wehani rice used in the stuffing has a chewy texture that I love. I cook it here with mushrooms in stock and eventually flavor it with leeks and onions.

By removing the chicken skin from the ballottine slices before they are served, you can eliminate about half the calories in the dish. Don't attempt to remove the skin from the whole ballottine before it is sliced, since it is essentially holding the chicken together. Rather, remove and discard the skin from each slice as it is cut. The ballottine is served with a rich wine sauce containing the defatted chicken drippings and finely diced vegetables (a brunoise).

FOR THE RED RICE STUFFING

1. Place the rice, stock, salt, and mushrooms in a large saucepan. Bring the mixture to a boil, cover, reduce the heat to low, and cook for 1 hour. Set the rice aside in the pan, uncovered, to cool.

2. Meanwhile, place the leek, onion, oil, and water in a saucepan. Bring the mixture to a boil, cover, reduce the heat to low, and cook at a gentle boil for 5 minutes. Remove the lid, and continue to cook until all the moisture is gone. Add the mixture to the pan containing the rice, mix well, and cool to room temperature.

RED WINE SAUCE

Drippings from cooking the
    chicken
½ cup water
½ cup red wine
1 stalk celery (2 ounces), peeled
    and cut into ¼-inch dice
    (½ cup)
1 small onion (3 ounces), peeled
    and chopped (½ cup)
1 carrot (2 ounces), peeled and
    cut into ¼-inch dice (⅓ cup)
½ teaspoon potato starch
    dissolved in 1 tablespoon
    water
1 tablespoon soy sauce
1 tablespoon chopped fresh
    parsley

FOR THE CHICKEN *BALLOTTINE*

3. Preheat the oven to 400 degrees.

4. Sprinkle the boned chicken with the salt and pepper, and stuff it with the cool rice mixture. Then roll the chicken up, tie it securely with string, and place it in a roasting pan. Roast the *ballottine* at 400 degrees for 1 hour, then lift it from the pan, and place it on a platter.

FOR THE WINE SAUCE

5. Remove and discard all fat from the drippings in the pan, and add the water and wine to the drippings. Heat the mixture, stirring to loosen and melt the solidified juices in the pan, and cook for 30 seconds. Strain into a saucepan, and add the celery, onion, and carrot. Bring the mixture to a boil over high heat. Cover, reduce the heat to low, and boil gently for 5 mintues. Stir in the dissolved potato starch and soy sauce, and bring the mixture back to a boil to thicken it.

6. Transfer the *ballottine* to a cutting board, cut half of it into four or five slices, each about 1 inch thick, and remove and discard the skin from each slice. Place the uncut half of the *ballottine* on the serving platter, and arrange the cut slices in front of it. Pour the wine sauce over and around the *ballottine,* and garnish with the parsley. Cut and skin additional slices of *ballottine* as needed at the table.

YIELD: 8 SERVINGS

Nutritional analysis per serving:

Calories 215	Fat 4.4 gm.
Protein 24 gm.	Saturated fat 0.1 gm.
Carbohydrates 16 gm.	Cholesterol 72 mg.
Sodium 377 mg.	

POACHED TURKEY IN VEGETABLE CONSOMMÉ

½ cup dry mushrooms (about ⅓ ounce)

7 cups (1¾ quarts) water

1 leek (6 ounces), trimmed (leaving most of the green parts), washed, and cut into ¼-inch dice (1¾ cups)

3 carrots (6 ounces), peeled and cut into ¼-inch dice (1 cup)

1 white turnip, peeled and cut into ¼-inch dice (1 cup)

2 ribs celery, cleaned and cut into ¼-inch dice (⅔ cup)

1 teaspoon salt

1 boneless turkey breast (2 pounds), skin removed

Crusty bread

Horseradish and hot mustard (optional)

YIELD: 4 SERVINGS

Nutritional analysis per serving:
Calories 262	Fat 1.5 gm.
Protein 46 gm.	Saturated fat 0.4 gm.
Carbohydrates 15 gm.	Cholesterol 111 mg.
Sodium 701 mg.	

Skinless, boneless turkey breasts are available now in most supermarkets around the country. Here, I cook a breast briefly in a flavorful vegetable stock composed of mushrooms, leek, carrots, turnip, celery, and water, then set the breast aside, covered, to finish cooking in the residual heat of the surrounding broth. This technique produces a very moist breast, which is a plus, since turkey breast meat is so lean that it tends to be dry if not properly cooked.

The turkey is sliced and served in soup bowls with the broth and vegetables. Horseradish and hot mustard, served on the side with some crusty bread, if desired, are good flavor enhancers. (See photograph, page 121.)

1. Place the mushrooms in a large pot with the water. Bring to a boil, and immediately remove the mushrooms, retaining the liquid in the pot. Chop the mushrooms coarsely, and return them to the pot.

2. Add all the remaining vegetables and the salt to the pot, bring the mixture to a boil, and boil gently for 5 minutes. Add the breast of turkey, and bring the mixture back to a boil. Reduce the heat, cover, and boil gently for 10 minutes. Remove the pot from the heat, and let the meat and vegetables stand in the hot broth, covered, for 30 minutes. Remove the turkey to a cutting board, and slice it.

3. Place one or two slices of the turkey breast in each of four soup bowls, ladle the hot broth with vegetables on top, and serve with crusty bread. Offer horseradish and hot mustard on the side, if desired. Or the turkey slices can be transferred to side plates to be eaten with the bread, mustard, and horseradish, while the broth and vegetables are consumed separately.

GRILLED PORK PAILLARDS WITH ROSEMARY

2 boneless pork fillets (about 1½ pounds), trimmed of all sinews and surrounding fat (trimmed weight about 1 pound)

3 tablespoons (loose) fresh rosemary leaves

¼ teaspoon whole black peppercorns

½ teaspoon salt

1 tablespoon corn or canola oil

YIELD: 4 SERVINGS

Nutritional analysis per serving:

Calories 169	Fat 7.4 gm.
Protein 24 gm.	Saturated fat 1.8 gm.
Carbohydrates 0.5 gm.	Cholesterol 74 mg.
Sodium 331 mg.	

 Paillard is the French name for a thin piece of meat— beef, veal, or pork—that is grilled or sautéed. The paillards here are made of lean, tender pork fillets, which I butterfly and pound to a thickness of ¼ inch, then lightly season and coat with oil. After brief cooking on a hot grill, the slices are transferred to a warm oven, where they "relax" and finish cooking in their own heat.

If you don't have access to a grill, first cook the paillards under a hot broiler, about 3 inches from the heat, for about 2 minutes a side before finishing them in the warm oven, as explained in the recipe.

1. Prewarm an oven to 160 or 170 degrees.

2. Cut the pork fillets in half crosswise, butterfly each of the four pieces, and pound them between sheets of plastic wrap to a thickness of ¼ inch.

3. Place the rosemary leaves, peppercorns, and salt in the bowl of a mini-chop or small grinder, and pulverize them. Sprinkle the pork with the seasoning mixture.

4. Pour the oil on a plate, and dip both sides of the *paillards* in the oil. Cook immediately, or stack the pieces of pork together on the plate, cover them with plastic wrap, and refrigerate them for up to 8 hours.

5. When you are ready to cook, heat a clean grill until very hot. Place the *paillards* on the grill, and cook them for about 1½ minutes on each side. (The meat should be undercooked at this point.) Arrange the pork on an ovenproof serving platter, and place it, uncovered, in the warm oven for at least 10 minutes and as long as 30 minutes, to "relax" and finish cooking in its own residual heat. Serve with the natural juices that have collected on the platter.

Garbure Soup Farmer-Style

1 boneless fully cooked smoked pork shoulder (about 2 pounds), trimmed of "skin" and surrounding fat (1½ pounds trimmed)

8 ounces dried white kidney beans

12 cups water

2 potatoes (12 ounces), peeled and cut into 1-inch pieces (1¾ cups)

1 leek (6 ounces), trimmed, washed, and cut into 1-inch pieces (2 cups), including most green portions

1 stalk celery (2 ounces), washed and cut into ½-inch pieces (1 cup)

Garbure is a soup from the southwest of France. Traditionally very rich, it often encompasses goose or duck confit *(pieces of duck or goose poached in their own fat), a variety of sausages, pork shoulder, and other types of meat, including pig's feet. I love garbure prepared in classical style, but I also enjoy this lighter version containing pork shoulder as the only meat.*

I trim the shoulder first, removing the "skin" and surrounding fat, then cook it with a selection of vegetables based on those in the original version. Served in the traditional manner with a layer of bread and crusty cheese on top, it makes a great main course. (See photograph, page 123.)

1. Place the pork in a large kettle, and add the beans and water. Bring the mixture to a boil over high heat, cover, reduce the heat to low, and boil gently for 1 hour.

2. Add the potatoes, leek, celery, carrots, parsnips, cabbage, and salt, and bring the mixture back to a boil. Cover, reduce the heat to low, and boil gently for 1 hour longer. By this time the meat will have separated into pieces. (You will have 4 quarts of soup. If you have less, add water to make 4 quarts.) To have 4 to 6 servings, reserve 2 quarts (8 cups) of the soup to use within the next 2 or 3 days, or freeze it for future use.

3. At serving time, preheat a broiler. Bring 2 quarts of the soup to a boil on top of the stove, and pour it into a 2½-quart casserole dish or enameled cast-iron pot. (The pot should be nearly full.) Arrange the bread slices on top to cover the soup in one layer, and push them gently into the liquid until they are moist.

3 carrots (6 ounces), peeled and cut into ½-inch pieces (1 cup)

3 parsnips (6 ounces), peeled and cut into ½-inch pieces (1 cup)

1 8-ounce piece savoy cabbage, cut into 2-inch pieces (4 cups)

About ½ teaspoon salt (depending on the saltiness of the pork)

4 thin (¼-inch) slices country bread (4 ounces)

1½ cups (lightly packed) grated swiss cheese (5 ounces), preferably Gruyère

4. Sprinkle the cheese on top, and place the dish under the hot broiler, about 4 inches from the heat. Broil for about 10 minutes, until the cheese on top is bubbly and brown. Carry the dish to the table, and serve in bowls or soup plates. You will have 4 to 6 servings.

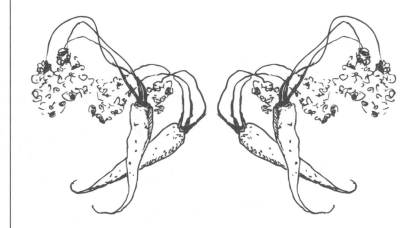

YIELD: 4 SERVINGS

Nutritional analysis per serving:

Calories 294	Fat 8.2 gm.
Protein 23 gm.	Saturated fat 3.8 gm.
Carbohydrates 33 gm.	Cholesterol 36 mg.
Sodium 769 mg.	

BARLEY-STUFFED CABBAGE ROLLS

½ cup pearl barley

9½ cups water

1 head savoy cabbage (about 1½ pounds)

1½ tablespoons canola oil

1 medium onion (about 7 ounces), peeled and chopped (1½ cups)

5 cloves garlic, peeled, crushed, and finely chopped (1 tablespoon)

4 tablespoons cider vinegar

1 pound lean ground beef (10 percent fat or less)

½ teaspoon freshly ground black pepper

½ teaspoon dried dill weed

½ teaspoon caraway seeds

½ teaspoon dried thyme leaves

CIDER-TOMATO SAUCE

1 cup tomato sauce

1½ cups homemade unsalted and defatted chicken stock (page 188) or lower-salt canned chicken broth

¼ teaspoon salt (less if using canned broth)

1 tablespoon brown sugar

2 tablespoons cider vinegar

Cooked barley lends body and texture to the stuffing for these savoy cabbage rolls, which are made with very lean ground beef. The rolls can be cooked ahead in the sweet-and-sour sauce and then reheated at serving time in a conventional or microwave oven.

1. Preheat the oven to 400 degrees.

2. Place the barley and 1½ cups of the water in a large saucepan. Bring the water to a boil, reduce the heat, cover, and boil the barley gently for 30 minutes, until it is tender. Set aside. Most of the water will be absorbed at this point.

3. Remove and reserve the core of the cabbage, and gently pull off nine or ten of the large outer leaves one at a time without tearing them. Bring the remaining 8 cups of water to a boil in a large pot. Drop the leaves into the water, and bring it back to a boil, gently pushing the leaves down under the water. Boil the leaves, covered, for 6 to 8 minutes, then drain them, and cool them under cold water. Remove the leaves from the water, shaking them gently to remove as much of the water clinging to them as possible, and set them aside.

4. Heat the oil in a large skillet. When it is hot, add the onion, and cook over medium to high heat, stirring occasionally, for 2 minutes. Trim the cabbage core, and cut it and the remaining cabbage leaves into ½-inch pieces. (You should have about 4 cups.) Add the garlic to the onion, stir well, and immediately add the cabbage heart pieces and vinegar. Cover, and cook over medium heat for 8 to 10 minutes, until the cabbage is wilted and tender and most of the moisture is gone from the pan. Cool.

5. When the cabbage mixture is cold, combine it in a bowl with the barley, ground beef, pepper, dill, caraway, and thyme.

6. Spread the reserved cabbage leaves on a flat work surface, and cut out and discard the thick part of the central rib in each. You will need eight of the leaves for stuffing; the remaining one or two leaves are for any patching that is necessary.

7. Divide the stuffing mixture among the eight leaves, and fold in the sides and ends of the leaves to enclose the stuffing. Place the stuffed leaves seam side down in a large gratin dish in one layer.

8. Combine the sauce ingredients in a saucepan, and bring the mixture to a boil. Pour the sauce over the cabbage rolls, cover the dish with aluminum foil, and bake at 400 degrees for 1 hour. Remove the foil, baste the rolls with the surrounding sauce, and continue baking them, uncovered, for 20 minutes, basting them once or twice more to create a nice glaze on top.

9. Run the dish under a hot broiler for a few minutes if you want the rolls browner on top, and serve them immediately, two rolls per person.

YIELD: 4 SERVINGS

Nutritional analysis per serving:

Calories 444	Fat 17.7 gm.
Protein 31 gm.	Saturated fat 5.1 gm.
Carbohydrates 45 gm.	Cholesterol 70 mg.
Sodium 691 mg.	

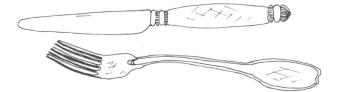

GRILLED LAMB CHOPS RIVIERA

7 teaspoons virgin olive oil

1 small onion (about 3 ounces), peeled and chopped (½ cup)

3 cloves garlic, peeled, crushed, and chopped (2 teaspoons)

1 pound spinach, trimmed of tough stems and washed (12 ounces trimmed)

1¼ teaspoons salt

½ teaspoon freshly ground black pepper

6 plum tomatoes (about 12 ounces), peeled, seeded, and cut into ½-inch pieces (1½ cups)

1 eggplant (about 1 pound), ends trimmed and remainder cut into 4 slices, each 1 inch thick

This dish is named Riviera because it is prepared in the style of the French Riviera, where tomatoes, egg-plant, and olives are common ingredients, along with spinach, which serves here as a base for the lamb chops. I pre-pare only one chop per person, selecting chops 1¾ inches thick with a trimmed weight of 6 ounces, which provides about 3 to 4 ounces of meat per serving.

I like the taste of grilled meat, so I cook these outside on a hot grill in summer. To use an oven, place them about 3 inches from the heat, and broil them for about 4 minutes on each side, then let them rest before serving, as instructed in the recipe. (See photograph, page 81.)

1. Preheat a grill. Preheat the oven to 350 degrees. Preheat a second oven to 160 degrees.

2. Heat 4 teaspoons of the olive oil in a large skillet. When the oil is hot, add the onion, and sauté it for 1 minute. Stir in the garlic, then add the spinach, ½ teaspoon of the salt, and ¼ teaspoon of the pepper. Cover and cook for 1 minute over high heat, just until the spinach wilts. Mix well, bringing the garlic and onions to the top so they don't burn, cover, and con-tinue cooking over medium heat for another 4 minutes. Transfer the spinach mixture to a bowl, and keep it warm until serving time.

3. Add the tomatoes to the unwashed skillet along with ¼ teaspoon of the salt. Cover, and cook for about 1 minute over medium heat, just long enough to heat through. Set aside, covered, until serving time.

4 loin lamb chops (about
2 pounds), each about
1¾ inches thick, trimmed of
all surrounding fat (about
1 pound, 8 ounces, trimmed)
16 oil-cured black olives

4. Sprinkle the eggplant slices with ¼ teaspoon of the salt, and brush them lightly on both sides with about 2½ teaspoons of the oil. Place the slices on the rack of the grill, and cook them for a total of 4 minutes, turning them once midway through, so they are nicely marked by the grill on both sides. Transfer the slices to a tray, and place them in the 350-degree oven for at least 10 minutes to finish cooking.

5. Meanwhile, sprinkle the lamb chops with the remaining ¼ teaspoon salt and ¼ teaspoon pepper. Brush them on both sides with the remaining ½ teaspoon oil, and place them on the rack of the grill. Cook them for a total of 7 to 8 minutes, turning them occasionally, until they are nicely browned on both sides. Arrange the chops on a tray, and place them in the 160-degree oven for at least 15 minutes and as long as 30 minutes, to finish cooking. (If your chops are thinner, cook them for proportionately less time.)

6. At serving time, spread the spinach on four warmed plates, and divide the tomatoes among the plates, sprinkling them on top of the spinach. Arrange a slice of eggplant in the center of each plate, and place a lamb chop on top of each slice. Place 4 olives on each plate. Spoon any natural juices from the lamb over the chops, and serve immediately.

YIELD: 4 SERVINGS

Nutritional analysis per serving:

Calories 352	Fat 19.3 gm.
Protein 30 gm.	Saturated fat 4.1 gm.
Carbohydrates 17 gm.	Cholesterol 81 mg.
Sodium 1,161 mg.	

Slow-Cooked Roast of Lamb

3½ pounds boneless leg of lamb roast, as lean as possible

5 to 6 cloves garlic, peeled, crushed, and chopped (1 tablespoon)

4 anchovy fillets, coarsely chopped

1 teaspoon *herbes de Provence* (see page 190)

½ teaspoon salt

1 tablespoon virgin olive oil

2 onions (12 ounces), peeled and cut into 1-inch pieces (2 cups)

½ cup water

1 tablespoon chopped fresh chives

YIELD: 8 SERVINGS

Nutritional analysis per serving:

Calories 290	Fat 10.9 gm.
Protein 42 gm.	Saturated fat 3.5 gm.
Carbohydrates 4 gm.	Cholesterol 128 mg.
Sodium 335 mg.	

Although I usually serve leg of lamb rare, I occasionally enjoy it slow-cooked until well done. Flavored with an anchovy-garlic mixture, the lamb is browned and then cooked slowly until tender on top of the stove in a Dutch oven or pot with a tight lid. This represents a different and delicious way of preparing leg of lamb.

1. If the lamb roast is rolled and tied, cut the string and unroll it; if it is not rolled, lay it as flat as possible. Trim off most of the fat and sinews. (The trimmed weight should be about 2¼ pounds.) Combine the garlic, anchovies, and *herbes de Provence* in a small bowl, and spread the mixture on what will be the interior of the roast after you roll it. Roll the roast up, and tie it securely with kitchen twine. Sprinkle the exterior of the roast with the salt.

2. Heat the oil in a cast-iron Dutch oven or similar pot with a tight lid. When the oil is hot, add the roast, and brown it over medium heat, partially covered (to prevent spattering), for 30 minutes, turning the meat occasionally with tongs so it browns evenly on all sides.

3. Add the onions and water, bring to a boil, cover the pan completely with the lid, and reduce the heat to very low. Continue to cook the roast for 2½ hours.

4. Pour the cooking liquid into a measuring cup. (You will have about 2 cups.) Let it rest for a few minutes, then scoop as much fat as possible from the top (about ⅓ cup). Return the remaining liquid to the pan containing the roast to serve as a natural sauce with the meat.

5. Cut the meat into slices, and arrange on a platter. Pour the sauce around and on top of the meat, and sprinkle with the chives. Serve.

VEAL CHOPS
WITH OLIVE SHAVINGS

1 tablespoon canola oil
4 veal chops (about 8 ounces each, ¾ inch thick), trimmed of as much surrounding fat as possible (about 7 ounces each trimmed)
¼ teaspoon salt
¼ teaspoon freshly ground black pepper
1 small onion (2 to 3 ounces), peeled and chopped (½ cup)
¼ cup dry white wine
⅓ cup water
1 tablespoon unsalted butter
1 tablespoon ketchup
8 ounces olives (a mixture of green, purple, and black varieties), pitted and cut into shavings (about 6 ounces)
1 tablespoon chopped fresh parsley or chives

If you take into account that the bone in each of these well-trimmed chops weighs an ounce or so, you end up with 5 to 6 ounces of meat per person in this dish, an adequate—but not excessive—amount. The chops are sautéed briefly, then finished in the oven. A sauce is created from the pan drippings, with the addition of a little onion, wine, water, butter, ketchup, and, finally, olive shavings.

1. Prewarm the oven to 180 degrees.

2. Heat the oil in a very large, sturdy skillet. Sprinkle the chops with the salt and pepper, and cook them in the hot oil over high heat for 3 minutes. Turn them over, and cook them on the other side for 3 minutes.

3. Remove the chops from the skillet (reserving the drippings), and place them on an ovenproof platter. Place the platter in the warm oven to allow the chops to "rest" while you make the sauce.

4. Add the onion to the drippings in the skillet, and sauté for 1½ minutes, stirring continuously. Add the wine, mix it in well, bring the mixture to a boil, and boil it for about 30 seconds. Add the water, butter, ketchup, and olive shavings, and boil for 1½ to 2 minutes.

5. Arrange the chops on individual plates, and spoon the sauce on top. Sprinkle with the parsley, and serve immediately.

YIELD: 4 SERVINGS

Nutritional analysis per serving:

Calories 307	Fat 16.5 gm.
Protein 32 gm.	Saturated fat 4.2 gm.
Carbohydrates 4 gm.	Cholesterol 133 mg.
Sodium 1,020 mg.	

SEARED CALVES' LIVER WITH TARRAGON-LEMON SAUCE

2 tablespoons unsalted butter

1 tablespoon virgin olive oil

½ teaspoon salt

½ teaspoon freshly ground black pepper

4 calves' liver steaks, each about ⅜ inch thick and 5 ounces (about 1¼ pounds total), cleaned of skin and as many sinews as possible

TARRAGON-LEMON SAUCE

½ cup coarsely chopped red onion

2 scallions, trimmed and finely minced (¼ cup)

2 tablespoons lemon juice

¼ cup water

1 tablespoon drained capers

2 teaspoons chopped fresh tarragon

YIELD: 4 SERVINGS

Nutritional analysis per serving:

Calories 384	Fat 15.4 gm.
Protein 26 gm.	Saturated fat 6.3 gm.
Carbohydrates 10 gm.	Cholesterol 454 mg.
Sodium 422 mg.	

For this dish, make sure that you buy calves' liver, which is much paler in color, milder in taste, and more flavorful than beef liver. I like my calves' liver pink inside—medium rare—and this is reflected in the recipe, but you can adjust the cooking time to your taste. After the steaks are cooked briefly in a skillet on top of the stove, they are transferred to a plate and set aside, covered, to finish cooking in their own residual heat, while a tarragon-and-lemon-flavored sauce is created from the liver drippings in the skillet.

1. Heat the butter and oil until hot in one very large (12-inch) or two smaller (8-inch) skillets. Sprinkle the salt and pepper on both sides of the liver steaks, and place them in the skillet(s) in one layer with no overlap. Sauté the steaks over high heat for about 1½ minutes on each side for medium rare (adjust the cooking time if your liver is thicker or thinner, or if you like it cooked more or less). Transfer the steaks to a plate, and cover them with an overturned plate. (They can wait like this for 10 to 15 minutes, while you prepare the sauce.)

FOR THE TARRAGON-LEMON SAUCE

2. Add the onion and scallions to the drippings in the skillet(s). Sauté for about 20 seconds, then add the lemon juice, and stir until all the solidified juices have melted. If you are using two skillets, at this point combine their contents in one, and boil the mixture for another 20 seconds, until most of the liquid has evaporated. Add the water, the capers, and the tarragon, mix well, and bring to a boil.

3. Arrange the liver steaks on individual plates, top with the tarragon-lemon sauce, and serve immediately.

TOP: GRATIN OF EGGPLANT AND TOMATO (SEE PAGE 126).
BOTTOM: HADDOCK STEAKS IN RICE PAPER WITH SHALLOT-AND-SOY SAUCE (SEE PAGE 65).

STEW OF LIMA BEANS AND MUSSELS WITH SPINACH (SEE PAGE 74).

SALMON IN ASPIC WITH HORSERADISH FLAKES (SEE PAGE 70).

TOP: STEAMED CAULIFLOWER WITH CHIVES (SEE PAGE 120).
BOTTOM: MONKFISH ROULADE WITH BITTER BROCCOLI STUFFING (SEE PAGE 68).

CHILI CON CARNE WITH RED BEANS

8 ounces dried red kidney beans

8 ounces very lean ground beef (10-percent fat or less)

1½ teaspoons salt

4 cups cold water

2 small or 1 medium onion (4 ounces), peeled and cut into 1-inch pieces (1½ cups)

6 scallions, trimmed, keeping most of the green, and cut into ½-inch pieces (1 cup)

5 to 6 cloves garlic, peeled, crushed, and chopped (1 tablespoon)

1 jalapeño pepper, seeded and chopped (2 teaspoons)

1 can (14 ounces) tomatoes in sauce

½ teaspoon dried thyme leaves

1 teaspoon ground cumin

1½ tablespoons chili powder

2 bay leaves

⅓ cup finely chopped cilantro stems

1 recipe Boiled Rice (see page 131)

⅓ cup (loose) coarsely chopped cilantro leaves

YIELD: 4 TO 6 SERVINGS

Nutritional analysis per serving (for 6):

Calories 344	Fat 4.8 gm.
Protein 20 gm.	Saturated fat 1.6 gm.
Carbohydrates 56 gm.	Cholesterol 23 mg.
Sodium 618 mg.	

 Real chili aficionados don't use beans, of course, in their renditions of this classic dish; in Texas, for example, meat—usually fatty beef, often from the shoulder—is the main ingredient. Beans are a prominent part of my chili, with meat used more as a seasoning. I select lean (10-percent fat) ground beef available now in supermarkets and extend the chili with red kidney beans. Notice that the beans and beef are cooked together first for an hour before the onions, scallions, garlic, jalapeño, and an assortment of herbs and spices are added; then the mixture is cooked for another hour. This gives the dish a fresher flavor, I think, than adding all the seasoning ingredients at the beginning. Spooned over Boiled Rice (see page 131), this soupy chili makes a satisfying one-dish meal for four or six people.

1. Sort through the beans, removing and discarding any damaged ones, and rinse in a sieve under cold water. Place the beans, beef, salt, and water in a stockpot, and bring the mixture to a boil over high heat. (This will take about 10 minutes.) Reduce the heat to low, cover, and boil gently for 1 hour.

2. Add the onions, scallions, garlic, jalapeño, tomatoes (with sauce), thyme, cumin, chili powder, bay leaves, and cilantro stems. Bring the mixture to a boil over high heat, reduce the heat to low, cover, and boil gently for 1 hour. (The mixture will still be somewhat soupy.)

3. To serve, spoon the chili over the rice, and sprinkle the cilantro leaves on top.

OSSO BUCO

- 4 10-ounce slices of veal shank with bones, each about 1½ inches thick (2½ pounds total, about half bones and half meat)
- 1 tablespoon unsalted butter
- 1 tablespoon virgin olive oil
- 1 medium onion (5 to 6 ounces), peeled and finely chopped (1¼ cups)
- 1 small leek (about 4 ounces), trimmed (with most green parts left on), coarsely chopped, and washed in a sieve (¾ cup)
- 1 medium carrot (3 ounces), trimmed, peeled, and coarsely chopped (½ cup)
- 6 cloves garlic, peeled, crushed, and finely chopped (4 teaspoons)
- 2 stalks celery (4 ounces), washed and coarsely chopped (⅔ cup)
- 1 teaspoon *herbes de Provence* (see page 190)
- ⅔ cup fruity white wine
- ⅔ cup water
- 1 teaspoon salt
- ½ teaspoon freshly ground black pepper
- 2 ripe medium tomatoes (10 to 11 ounces), halved, seeded, and cut into ½-inch pieces (1¼ cups)

Osso buco literally means "bone with a hole" (or "with a mouth") in Italian. It is a reference to the large bones that are about half the content of the slices of veal shank traditionally used as the main ingredient in this classic dish. I brown the meat in the standard way in a large, sturdy pot, then add wine, water, and a multitude of garnishes, and cook the dish slowly until the veal is very tender. At the end, the osso buco is flavored with grated orange and lemon rind, and shredded basil leaves are sprinkled on top. Quite delicious, it goes particularly well with Brown Saffron Rice (see page 132).

1. Pat the veal dry with paper towels. Heat the butter and oil in a large, sturdy saucepan or Dutch oven. When they are hot, add the meat in one layer, and brown it over medium to high heat on all sides for about 12 minutes. Add the onion, leek, and carrot, mix well, and cook for 2 minutes. Then add the garlic, celery, *herbes de Provence,* wine, water, salt, and pepper, mix well, and bring the mixture to a strong boil. Reduce the heat to low, cover, and cook gently for 1½ hours, until the meat is tender when pierced with the point of a sharp knife.

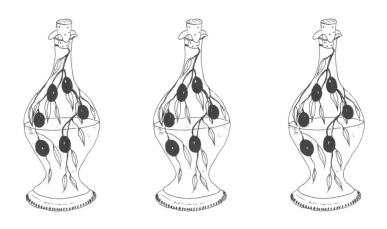

1 tablespoon grated orange
  rind
1 tablespoon grated lemon rind
1 teaspoon potato starch or
  cornstarch dissolved in
  1 tablespoon white wine
½ cup shredded fresh basil
  leaves

2. Add the tomato, orange rind, and lemon rind, mix well, and bring back to a boil. Boil, uncovered, for 2 to 3 minutes. Add the dissolved starch mixture, and bring to a boil again. Remove the pan from the heat, add the basil, mix gently, cover, and set aside until ready to serve. (The dish is more flavorful if allowed to sit for at least 30 minutes before serving. It can be made up to 8 hours ahead and reheated, with the basil added at the time of reheating.)

3. Serve a slice of shank with bone to each person. Pour sauce over and around the shanks, and serve them with Brown Saffron Rice (see page 132).

YIELD: 4 SERVINGS

Nutritional analysis per serving:

Calories 280	Fat 9.2 gm.
Protein 33 gm.	Saturated fat 3.0 gm.
Carbohydrates 16 gm.	Cholesterol 118 mg.
Sodium 687 mg.	

Daube of Beef Arlésienne

- 8 small red potatoes (about 8 ounces), peeled
- 1½ cups water
- 8 small pearl onions (about 5 ounces), peeled
- About 12 to 16 baby carrots (4 ounces), peeled
- 1½ teaspoons virgin olive oil
- 4 boned shoulder blade beef steaks or chicken steaks, trimmed of all surrounding fat and cut in half (20 to 24 ounces total trimmed weight)
- 1 medium onion (about 5 ounces), peeled and chopped (1 cup)
- 1 cup dry white wine
- 1¼ teaspoons salt
- 1 teaspoon *herbes de Provence* (see page 190)

This dish comes from Arles, the small town in Provence made famous by Vincent van Gogh. A beef stew, the daube *is flavored with small potatoes, pearl onions, baby carrots, white wine, and herbes de Provence. I like to use shoulder blade steaks (sometimes called chicken steaks) in this dish, because they are very lean, except for a strip of nerve tissue in the center that becomes gelatinous as the meat cooks and keeps it moist and flavorful.*

A mixture of hazelnuts, toasted bread, garlic, and parsley is transformed into a powder and added to the dish just before it is served. Other last minute additions are capers, olives, and tomatoes, ingredients that are special to the Provence region of France.

1. Place the potatoes and water in a saucepan, and bring to a boil over high heat. Cover the pan, reduce the heat to low, and boil the potatoes gently for 8 minutes.

2. Add the pearl onions and carrots, bring the mixture back to a boil over high heat, cover, reduce the heat to low, and boil gently for another 8 minutes, or until all the vegetables are tender but still firm when pierced with the point of a sharp knife. Drain off and reserve the vegetable cooking liquid (you should have about 1½ cups), and set the vegetables aside in the pan.

3. Heat the oil in a large, sturdy pot. When it is hot, add the steaks and cook them over medium to high heat for 8 to 10 minutes, turning them once midway through, so they are browned on both sides. Add the chopped onion, and cook it with the steaks for 2 minutes, stirring occasionally. Then mix in the reserved vegetable cooking liquid, white wine, salt, and *herbes de Provence.* Bring the mixture to a boil, cover, reduce

ARLÉSIENNE MIXTURE

- **2** tablespoons shelled hazelnuts
- **1** slice toasted country bread (about 1 ounce)
- **2** cloves garlic, peeled
- **½** cup (loose) fresh parsley leaves
- **2** tablespoons drained capers
- **¼** cup *Niçoise* olives
- **1** medium tomato (6 ounces), seeded and cut into 1-inch dice (¾ cup)

the heat to very low, and boil very gently for 1 hour. (The recipe can be prepared to this point a day ahead.)

FOR THE *ARLÉSIENNE* MIXTURE

4. Preheat the oven to 400 degrees.

5. Spread the hazelnuts on a tray, and toast them at 400 degrees for 10 minutes. Place the bread, hazelnuts, garlic, and parsley in the bowl of food processor, and process the mixture until it is finely chopped.

6. At serving time, add the bread and hazelnut mixture along with the reserved vegetables to the beef mixture in the pot. Mix well, bring the *daube* to a boil, and cook it gently for 5 minutes to heat it through completely. Add the capers, olives, and tomato, cook 1 additional minute, and serve immediately.

YIELD: 4 SERVINGS

Nutritional analysis per serving:

Calories 389	Fat 16.9 gm.
Protein 34 gm.	Saturated fat 4.9 gm.
Carbohydrates 25 gm.	Cholesterol 101 mg.
Sodium 1,058 mg.	

VENISON STEAKS IN SWEET-SOUR SAUCE

1 loin of venison (about 1½ pounds), completely trimmed of fat (about 1 pound trimmed)
1 teaspoon canola oil
1 teaspoon chopped fresh thyme leaves
1 tablespoon ketchup
1 tablespoon currant jelly or seedless raspberry jam
2 teaspoons soy sauce
¼ cup cold water
1 tablespoon peanut oil
1 tablespoon unsalted butter
¼ teaspoon salt
¼ teaspoon freshly ground black pepper
1 tablespoon chopped shallots
2 tablespoons red wine vinegar

Be sure to obtain your venison from a reputable source, so you know that the meat has been aged and is tender. Thoroughly trimmed of fat, the steaks are very lean, quite flavorful, and rich, so 4 to 5 ounces of meat per person are adequate. Venison is traditionally served with a sweet-sour sauce. The sauce I have created here contains currant jelly for sweetness, and vinegar—cooked with shallots and added to the sauce at the end—for a contrasting sour taste. I particularly enjoy this main course served with Skillet Sweet Potatoes (recipe on page 130). (See photograph, page 84.)

1. Cut the trimmed loin into four steaks, each about 4 ounces. Pound the steaks gently until each is about ¾ inch thick. Rub the steaks with the canola oil, and sprinkle them with the thyme. Arrange the steaks in a single layer on a plate, cover with plastic wrap, and refrigerate for at least 1 hour and as long as 8 hours before cooking.

2. Mix the ketchup, jelly, soy sauce, and water together in a small bowl, and set aside.

3. When you are ready to cook the steaks, prewarm the oven to 180 degrees.

4. Heat the peanut oil and butter until hot in a large, sturdy saucepan. Sprinkle the steaks with the salt and pepper, place them in the saucepan, and sauté over medium to high heat for 2 to 2½ minutes on each side for medium-rare meat. Transfer the steaks to an ovenproof plate (retaining the drippings in the pan), cover with aluminum foil, and keep warm in the oven while you make the sauce.

5. Add the shallots to the drippings in the pan, and sauté them for about 20 seconds. Add the vinegar, and cook until most of the moisture has evaporated (about 1½ minutes). Add the jelly mixture, and mix well. Boil for 10 seconds, and strain through a fine mesh strainer.

6. Place each steak on a plate, coat with some of the sauce, and serve immediately with Skillet Sweet Potatoes (see page 130).

YIELD: 4 SERVINGS

Nutritional analysis per serving:

Calories 224	Fat 10.1 gm.
Protein 26 gm.	Saturated fat 3.5 gm.
Carbohydrates 5 gm.	Cholesterol 104 mg.
Sodium 412 mg.	

Pan-Seared or Grilled Marinated Flank Steak

HONEY-CORIANDER MARINADE

- 1 tablespoon honey
- 2 tablespoons soy sauce
- 5 to 6 cloves garlic, peeled, crushed, and finely chopped (1 tablespoon)
- ½ teaspoon ground coriander seeds
- ¼ teaspoon cayenne pepper

- 1 flank steak (about ¾ inch thick, weighing about 1¼ pounds), trimmed of all surrounding fat

YIELD: 4 SERVINGS

Nutritional analysis per serving:

Calories 246	Fat 10.8 gm.
Protein 30 gm.	Saturated fat 4.7 gm.
Carbohydrates 6 gm.	Cholesterol 71 mg.
Sodium 604 mg.	

For this recipe, a well-trimmed flank steak is grilled briefly, then finished in a 180-degree oven. I like my steak medium rare, and this recipe reflects my preference; if you prefer your meat more well done, however, simply cook it longer. Ideally, the steak should be cooked on the clean rack of a very hot grill. If this is not possible, cook it on top of the stove in a heavy aluminum or cast-iron pan, since both of these have good heat transfer. Don't use a nonstick pan here; those pans don't react well to extremely high temperatures.

The steak can be marinated for up to a day before it is cooked. The marinade, a mixture of honey, soy sauce, garlic, coriander, and cayenne pepper, can be altered to suit individual tastes. (See photograph, page 82.)

1. Mix all the marinade ingredients together in a gratin dish large enough to hold the flank steak. Place the steak in the dish, turning it to coat all sides with the marinade. Cover with plastic wrap, and marinate in the refrigerator for at least 1 hour.

2. At cooking time, heat a grill until very hot, or preheat a heavy aluminum or cast-iron skillet or saucepan for at least 5 minutes over high heat, until it is very hot. Prewarm the oven to 180 degrees.

3. Remove the steak, reserving the marinade in the gratin dish. Place the steak on the hot grill or skillet, cook over high heat for 1½ minutes, turn, and cook for 1½ minutes on the second side to sear the meat and give it a well-browned exterior. Return the meat to the marinade, and place it, uncovered, in the warm oven to "relax" and continue cooking in its own heat for at least 10 minutes and up to 40 minutes.

4. To serve, cut the steak on the diagonal into very thin (⅛-inch) slices, and serve with the marinade on very hot plates.

SIDE DISHES

ARUGULA AND OLIVE SALAD

About 14 ounces arugula

20 oil-cured black olives

2 slices firm-textured white bread (2 ounces)

1½ teaspoons virgin olive oil

LEMON DRESSING

1½ tablespoons lemon juice

2 tablespoons virgin olive oil

¼ teaspoon salt

⅛ teaspoon freshly ground black pepper

Nutritional analysis per serving:

Calories 161	Fat 13.3 gm.
Protein 3 gm.	Saturated fat 1.7 gm.
Carbohydrates 9 gm.	Cholesterol 0 mg.
Sodium 637 mg.	

 Arugula, called roquette in France and sometimes rocket in this country, is a pungent, garlicky salad green that goes particularly well with the lemon dressing in this recipe. You can, however, substitute other greens if arugula is not available, combining them with the dressing in the same manner and serving the salad garnished with olives and croutons. (See photograph, page 47.)

1. Preheat the oven to 400 degrees.

2. Wash the arugula, removing and discarding the tough outer leaves and stems. Dry it thoroughly, taking care not to bruise the leaves. (You should have 8 lightly packed cups.)

3. Pit the olives and cut them into ½-inch pieces. (You should have ½ cup.)

4. Trim the crusts from the bread slices, and cut the bread into ½-inch cubes. (You should have 1¼ cups.) Place the bread cubes in a bowl, add the 1½ teaspoons of olive oil, and rub the oil gently into the cubes to coat them well. Arrange the cubes on a baking tray, and bake them at 400 degrees for 8 minutes, until they are well browned. Set aside.

FOR THE LEMON DRESSING

5. In a bowl large enough to hold the arugula greens, mix all the dressing ingredients.

6. At serving time, add the arugula to the bowl containing the dressing, and toss well to combine. Divide the arugula among four plates, and sprinkle the olives and croutons on top and around the greens. Serve immediately.

Romaine with Creamy Yogurt Dressing

1 tablespoon white wine
vinegar

¼ teaspoon salt

¼ teaspoon freshly ground
black pepper

3 tablespoons nonfat plain
yogurt

1 tablespoon virgin olive oil

8 to 10 ounces romaine lettuce,
ribs cut in half and leaves torn
into 1½- to 2-inch pieces
(6 cups)

1 tablespoon chopped fresh
herb mixture (tarragon,
chives, basil, and chervil)

Romaine lettuce holds up particularly well to a light dressing that substitutes plain, nonfat yogurt for most of the oil. Cool and tangy, the yogurt gives the dressing a creamy consistency and a refreshingly sour taste that makes it a good accompaniment for Chili con Carne with Red Beans (see page 105).

1. In a bowl large enough to hold the lettuce, whisk together the vinegar, salt, pepper, and yogurt. Whisk in the oil.

2. Wash the lettuce pieces well in cold water and spin them dry in a salad spinner.

3. Add the lettuce to the dressing in the bowl, and toss it until coated with the dressing. Sprinkle on the fresh herbs, and serve immediately.

YIELD: 4 SERVINGS

Nutritional analysis per serving:

Calories 47	Fat 3.5 gm.
Protein 2 gm.	Saturated fat 0.5 gm.
Carbohydrates 3 gm.	Cholesterol 0.2 mg.
Sodium 148 mg.	

SAUTÉED HARICOTS VERTS AND SHALLOTS

1½ cups water
1 pound *haricots verts* (very thin French green beans), or very small regular string beans, tips removed
1 tablespoon unsalted butter
1 tablespoon peanut oil
2 shallots, peeled and finely chopped (2 tablespoons)
¼ teaspoon salt
¼ teaspoon freshly ground black pepper

Try to find authentic haricots verts, thin French green beans—sometimes available in specialty food stores or at farmers' markets—for this classic dish. If these are impossible to locate, however, cook the smallest, firmest regular string beans you can find until they are tender but still firm, and finish them with sautéed shallots and seasonings. (See photograph, page 83.)

1. Bring the water to a boil in a large saucepan. Rinse the beans, and add them to the boiling water. Cook, covered, over high heat for 7 or 8 minutes, until the beans are tender but still firm to the bite. Drain the beans (most of the water will have evaporated), and spread them on a large platter to cool.

2. At serving time, heat the butter and oil in a skillet. When they are hot, add the shallots, and sauté for about 10 seconds. Add the beans, salt, and pepper, and continue to sauté for about 2 minutes, until the beans are heated through. Serve with Grilled Chicken with Tarragon Butter (see page 80), if desired.

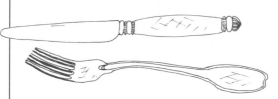

YIELD: 4 SERVINGS

Nutritional analysis per serving:
Calories 90
Protein 2 gm.
Carbohydrates 8 gm.
Sodium 142 mg.
Fat 6.4 gm.
Saturated fat 2.4 gm.
Cholesterol 8 mg.

FLAGEOLETS IN MIREPOIX

½ pound dried flageolets

1 small onion (3 ounces), peeled and chopped (½ cup)

1 carrot (2 ounces), peeled and cut into ¼-inch dice (⅓ cup)

1 small rib celery (1½ ounces), peeled and cut into ¼-inch dice (⅓ cup)

1 piece leek (2 ounces), white and green parts thinly sliced (½ cup) and washed under cold water in a sieve

½ teaspoon *herbes de Provence* (see page 190)

1½ cups homemade unsalted and defatted chicken stock (see page 188) or lower-salt canned chicken broth

1½ cups water

1 teaspoon salt (less if using canned broth)

1 tomato, seeded and cut into ½-inch dice (¾ cup)

1 tablespoon virgin olive oil

Flageolets are a French bean variety. Although you can occasionally find them fresh here, they are more likely to be available dried and can usually be found in specialty food stores. Long and narrow, they are light green in color because they are picked when only half ripe. They look somewhat like small dried lima beans and take about the same length of time to cook. I cook them here with finely diced vegetables (mirepoix) that add flavor. A traditional lamb accompaniment, flageolets go very well with Slow-Cooked Roast of Lamb (see page 98).

1. Wash the flageolets, removing and discarding any stones or foreign matter, and place them in a pot with all the rest of the ingredients except the tomato and the oil. Bring the mixture to a boil, cover, reduce the heat to low, and boil gently for about 1½ hours, until the beans are tender and most of the liquid has evaporated.

2. Using a hand blender in the pot, puree a small amount of the mixture (or remove a cup of the beans, puree them in a food processor or mini-chop, and add the puree to the pot). Stir the puree into the pot to thicken the whole mixture slightly.

3. Stir in the tomato and oil, and serve immediately, or cool, cover, refrigerate, and reheat for later serving.

YIELD: 4 GENEROUS SERVINGS

Nutritional analysis per serving:

Calories 268

Protein 13 gm.

Carbohydrates 44 gm.

Sodium 632 mg.

Fat 5.3 gm.

Saturated fat 0.7 gm.

Cholesterol 0 mg.

DRIED LIMA BEAN PUREE

4 ounces large dried lima beans

1½ cups homemade unsalted and defatted chicken stock (see page 188), lower-salt canned chicken broth, or water

⅓ teaspoon salt (less if using canned chicken broth)

⅛ teaspoon *herbes de Provence* (see page 190)

1 tablespoon virgin olive oil

 Dried lima beans cook quickly and are very good pureed. I cook them here in chicken stock flavored with a little salt and herbes de Provence, *although you can substitute water for the stock if you want a vegetarian dish. When tender, the beans are transformed into a smooth, delicate puree in a food processor.*

The puree can be prepared ahead. Reheat it, however, in a double boiler or microwave oven, since it tends to burn if warmed conventionally on top of the stove in a saucepan.

1. Wash the lima beans, and sort through them, removing and discarding any pebbles or damaged beans. Place the beans, stock, salt, and *herbes de Provence* in a saucepan, and bring the mixture to a boil over high heat. Then cover the pan, reduce the heat to low, and cook the beans gently for about 35 minutes, until they are soft and tender. There should be only a little liquid remaining in the pan.

2. Transfer the beans and liquid to the bowl of a food processor, and process the mixture for 15 to 20 seconds. Add the oil, and process for a few seconds, until it is incorporated.

3. Serve immediately, or set aside and reheat at serving time in a double boiler or microwave oven.

YIELD: 4 SERVINGS

Nutritional analysis per serving:

Calories 139	Fat 4.1 gm.
Protein 7 gm.	Saturated fat 0.6 gm.
Carbohydrates 19 gm.	Cholesterol 0 mg.
Sodium 239 mg.	

STEAMED CAULIFLOWER WITH CHIVES

1 firm, white cauliflower, trimmed of all green leaves (1½ pounds)
3 cups water
¼ teaspoon salt
¼ teaspoon freshly ground black pepper
1 tablespoon unsalted butter
1 tablespoon peanut oil
¼ cup minced fresh chives

Especially flavorful if prepared at the last moment, this dish features florets of cauliflower that are steamed and then tossed with a little butter, peanut oil, chives, salt, and pepper. Be sure to use firm, white cauliflower for this dish. Older specimens with dark spots on top have a much stronger flavor. (See photograph, page 104.)

1. Wash the cauliflower, and divide it into 12 to 16 florets of approximately equal size.

2. Bring the water to a boil in the base of a steamer or pot, preferably stainless steel. Place a steamer basket in the pot, add the cauliflower florets, cover, and cook over medium to high heat for about 10 minutes, until the florets are tender but still firm.

3. Transfer the cauliflower to a serving bowl, add the salt, pepper, butter, peanut oil, and chives, and toss briefly to mix. Serve immediately.

YIELD: 4 SERVINGS

Nutritional analysis per serving:

Calories 72	Fat 6.4 gm.
Protein 1 gm.	Saturated fat 2.4 gm.
Carbohydrates 3 gm.	Cholesterol 8 mg.
Sodium 146 mg.	

POACHED TURKEY IN VEGETABLE CONSOMMÉ (SEE PAGE 90).

TOP: POTATO AND SPINACH *GALETTE* (SEE PAGE 76). BOTTOM: CHICKEN *CHASSEUR* (SEE PAGE 85).

GARBURE SOUP FARMER-STYLE (SEE PAGE 92) WITH ASSORTED BREADS (SEE PAGES 182-87).

CLOCKWISE FROM TOP: PEARS IN GRENADINE (SEE PAGE 146); APRICOT *DÉLICE* (SEE PAGE 149); BROILED FIGS IN PEACH SAUCE (SEE PAGE 147).

CELERIAC AND POTATO PUREE

1 celeriac (about 1 pound, 6 ounces)
1¼ pounds potatoes
1¼ cups water
¾ teaspoon salt
1 tablespoon unsalted butter
¾ cup milk

 Although of the same family as celery stalks, celeriac is a different vegetable entirely, with a flavor almost too intense to enjoy on its own. I cook it here with potatoes and then puree the vegetables together. The result is delightful.

1. Peel the celeriac and cut it into 2-inch chunks. Peel the potatoes, wash them, and cut them into 2-inch chunks.

2. Place the celeriac and potatoes in a saucepan with the water and ¼ teaspoon of the salt. Bring to a boil, reduce the heat, cover, and boil the vegetables gently until tender, about 30 minutes.

3. Push the vegetables and their cooking liquid through a food mill set over a saucepan. Whisk in the butter, then add the remaining salt and the milk, and whisk them into the puree. Serve hot.

YIELD: 4 SERVINGS (4 TO 5 CUPS)

Nutritional analysis per serving:
Calories 190
Protein 6 gm.
Carbohydrates 34 gm.
Sodium 576 mg.
Fat 4.9 gm.
Saturated fat 2.8 gm.
Cholesterol 14 mg.

GRATIN OF EGGPLANT AND TOMATO

2 long, narrow, firm eggplants (1 pound total)

2 tablespoons corn oil

½ teaspoon salt

1 slice fine-textured white bread, processed into crumbs in a food processor (⅔ cup)

⅓ cup grated parmesan cheese

1 teaspoon chopped fresh thyme leaves

1 tablespoon virgin olive oil

4 ripe medium tomatoes (about 1 pound), cut into ⅜-inch slices

YIELD: 4 SERVINGS

Nutritional analysis per serving:

Calories 194	Fat 12.9 gm.
Protein 6 gm.	Saturated fat 2.7 gm.
Carbohydrates 16 gm.	Cholesterol 6 mg.
Sodium 448 mg.	

To begin this dish, lightly oiled slices of eggplant are spread on a tray and baked. Far easier than cooking them the conventional way (in batches in a skillet), this approach is healthier, too, since much less oil is required. The slices are then layered with tomatoes in a gratin dish, topped with flavored bread crumbs, and finished in the oven. (See photograph, page 101.)

1. Preheat the oven to 400 degrees.

2. Trim (but do not peel) the eggplants, and cut them lengthwise into ½-inch slices. (You will have about eight slices.)

3. Coat the bottom of a jelly roll pan or roasting pan with the corn oil. Lay the eggplant slices in a single layer in the oiled pan, and then immediately turn them over in the pan so they are lightly oiled on both sides.

4. Sprinkle the slices with the salt, and bake them for 15 minutes. Then turn the slices carefully with a large metal spatula (they will be soft), and bake them for another 10 minutes. Set the eggplant aside in the pan, and let it cool to lukewarm.

5. Meanwhile, in a small bowl, mix the bread crumbs, parmesan cheese, thyme, and olive oil.

6. Arrange alternating slices of eggplant and tomato in a 4- to 6-cup gratin dish, overlapping the slices as required to fit them all into the dish. Sprinkle the bread crumb mixture evenly on top. (At this point, the dish can be covered and refrigerated for up to 8 hours.)

7. When ready to cook the gratin, preheat the oven to 400 degrees. Bake the gratin for 20 to 25 minutes, until the vegetables are soft and heated through, and the crumb topping is nicely browned. Serve immediately.

CARAMELIZED MUSHROOMS WITH SHALLOTS

1½ tablespoons virgin olive oil
1 pound mushrooms, preferably older specimens, with slightly opened and darkened gills, washed
3 to 4 shallots (3 ounces), peeled and thinly sliced (1 cup)
1 tablespoon unsalted butter
⅓ cup chopped fresh flat-leaf parsley
½ teaspoon salt
½ teaspoon freshly ground black pepper

 I like to use medium to large mushrooms in this recipe, preferring the older, somewhat darker specimens with visible gills because they are more flavorful. To achieve the concentrated taste I want here, I cook the mushrooms for a long time—it takes a while for the moisture to emerge from them and evaporate, and then for them to brown. When done, the mushrooms are almost meatlike in texture and have an intense flavor that is further enhanced by the addition of shallots and parsley. (See photograph, page 82.)

1. Heat the oil in a skillet with a lid. When it is hot, add the mushrooms, and cook them, covered, over medium heat for 20 to 25 minutes, until all the liquid that emerges from them has disappeared and the mushrooms are nicely browned.

2. Add the shallots to the skillet, and sauté them, uncovered, for 2 to 3 minutes, until they are soft and brown.

3. Add the butter, parsley, salt, and pepper, and sauté for 10 seconds longer. Serve immediately.

YIELD: 4 SERVINGS

Nutritional analysis per serving:

Calories 114	Fat 8.4 gm.
Protein 3 gm.	Saturated fat 2.5 gm.
Carbohydrates 9 gm.	Cholesterol 8 mg.
Sodium 283 mg.	

BUTTERED POTATOES WITH PARSLEY

1½ pounds potatoes, peeled and cut into 2-inch pieces (about 20 pieces)

1½ tablespoons unsalted butter

¼ teaspoon salt

3 tablespoons chopped fresh parsley

 A time-honored combination, potatoes with parsley are always welcome. Trim the potato pieces to form ovals of nearly equal size, then boil them in water until tender. After the water is discarded, return the potatoes to the stove briefly to eliminate any remaining moisture—a simple step that produces potatoes with a creamy, smooth interior. Finish the dish with butter, salt, and parsley.

1. Trim the potato pieces (reserving the trimmings for soup, if desired), rounding them off to make ovals of about the same size and shape. Rinse the potato pieces well, place them in a saucepan, and add enough cold tap water to cover. Bring to a boil, reduce the heat to low, and boil gently for 15 to 20 minutes.

2. Drain the water, and place the saucepan containing the potatoes back on the stove over high heat for about 30 seconds to evaporate any remaining moisture from the potatoes. (This step is important, as it will give you a very moist and smooth-textured potato.)

3. Add the butter, salt, and parsley, toss gently (to avoid breaking the potatoes), and serve immediately.

YIELD: 4 SERVINGS

Nutritional analysis per serving:

Calories 140	Fat 4.4 gm.
Protein 3 gm.	Saturated fat 2.7 gm.
Carbohydrates 23 gm.	Cholesterol 12 mg.
Sodium 144 mg.	

POTATO GAUFRETTES OR CHIPS

3 tablespoons canola oil
1 large white or sweet potato (about 12 ounces), peeled and cut into about 20 waferlike slices on a mandoline, or into paper-thin slices in a food processor fitted with the slicing disk
⅛ teaspoon salt

There are two possible recipes here: Large potatoes can be cut either into waferlike slices on a mandoline to make gaufrettes, or—using the slicing disk on a food processor—into paper-thin slices for chips. Instead of frying the potatoes in a deep fryer, where they would absorb a great deal of oil, I arrange the slices on an oiled tray and bake them in the oven. Much lower in calories than conventional gaufrettes or chips, they make a great meat accompaniment or a good snack on their own. (See photograph, page 81.)

1. Preheat the oven to 400 degrees.

2. Coat the bottom of a jelly roll pan with 2 tablespoons of the oil. Arrange a single layer of the sliced potatoes in the pan so they fit snugly against one another. Then turn the slices over once in the oil (so they are lightly oiled on both sides).

3. Place the pan in the hot oven for 16 to 18 mintues, until the potato slices are dry and nicely browned. (Some of the slices will brown faster than others; as they brown, carefully remove them with a spatula.) Place the slices on a rack to cool.

4. Repeat with the rest of the potato slices, replenishing the tray with the remaining tablespoon of oil as needed.

5. Lightly salt the *gaufrettes* or chips, and serve.

YIELD: 4 SERVINGS

Nutritional analysis per serving:
Calories 141   Fat 10.3 gm.
Protein 1 gm.   Saturated fat 0.8 gm.
Carbohydrates 11 gm.   Cholesterol 0 mg.
Sodium 73 mg.

SKILLET SWEET POTATOES

1 large sweet potato (about
 1 pound), peeled and cut
 crosswise into 12 slices, each
 about ¼ inch thick
1 tablespoon unsalted butter
1 tablespoon corn oil
½ cup water
¼ teaspoon salt

For this recipe, I like to use bright orange yam slices, beginning them in a mixture of butter, oil, and water, then continuing to cook them until nicely browned after the water has evaporated. An easy dish, it is good with almost any meat or fish main course. (See photograph, page 84.)

1. Arrange the potato slices in a single layer in one very large or two slightly smaller nonstick skillets. Add the butter, oil, water, and salt. Bring the mixture to a boil, cover, and boil gently over high heat for about 5 minutes. Most of the water will have evaporated, and the potatoes will be soft.

2. Continue to cook, uncovered, over medium heat, turning until the slices are nicely browned on both sides, about 1 additional minute per side. Serve immediately.

YIELD: 4 SERVINGS

Nutritional analysis per serving:

Calories 141	Fat 6.5 gm.
Protein 1 gm.	Saturated fat 2.3 gm.
Carbohydrates 20 gm.	Cholesterol 8 mg.
Sodium 146 mg.	

BOILED RICE

2 cups water
¼ teaspoon salt
1 cup long-grain white rice

Simply boiled in salted water, long-grain white rice is useful as a garnish for any type of stew, some soups, and Chili con Carne with Red Beans (see page 105). Some varieties of rice are stickier than others. If you prefer a sticky rice—and many people do—whether for serving as a side dish or as the base for a rice pudding, use a rice that is not converted.

1. Bring the water and salt to a boil in a large saucepan. Add the rice, mix well, and bring back to a boil. Then reduce the heat to low, cover, and boil gently for 20 minutes.

2. Fluff the rice with a fork, and serve immediately.

YIELD: 4 SERVINGS

Nutritional analysis per serving:

Calories 167	Fat 0.3 gm.
Protein 3 gm.	Saturated fat 0.1 gm.
Carbohydrates 37 gm.	Cholesterol 0 mg.
Sodium 137 mg.	

BROWN SAFFRON RICE

2 teaspoons unsalted butter

2 teaspoons peanut oil

1 small onion or piece of large onion (about 2 ounces), peeled and finely chopped (⅓ cup)

6 to 7 ounces short-grain brown rice (1 cup)

½ teaspoon dried thyme

2¼ cups homemade unsalted and defatted chicken stock (see page 188) or lower-salt canned chicken broth

¼ teaspoon salt (less if using canned broth)

1½ teaspoons dried saffron

¼ cup grated parmesan cheese

Although you conventionally need about twice as much liquid as rice by volume, the ratios vary more widely with brown rice varieties, which also take longer to cook than white rice. The cup of short-grain brown rice I use for this recipe requires 2¼ cups of liquid and takes 45 minutes to cook, but you should make adjustments when preparing this dish to accommodate the peculiarities of the brown rice you are using.

1. Heat the butter and oil in a sturdy saucepan. When they are hot, add the onion, and sauté for 1 minute over medium heat. Add the rice, thyme, stock, salt, and saffron, and mix well.

2. Bring the mixture to a full boil, stirring occasionally, over high heat. Then reduce the heat to very low, cover, and cook at a very gentle boil for about 45 minutes (some varieties may cook faster than others), until the rice is tender, slightly sticky, and still somewhat chewy. Add the grated cheese, and mix it gently into the rice with the tines of a fork.

3. Serve the rice with Osso Buco (see page 106).

YIELD: 4 SERVINGS

Nutritional analysis per serving:

Calories 257   Fat 7.9 gm.
Protein 7 gm.   Saturated fat 3.0 gm.
Carbohydrates 39 gm. Cholesterol 9 mg.
Sodium 311 mg.

Red Swiss Chard with Ginger

1¼ pounds small red Swiss chard
3 tablespoons virgin olive oil
4 large shallots (about 4 ounces), peeled and finely chopped (½ cup)
1 1½-ounce piece of ginger, peeled and finely chopped (2 tablespoons)
1 small jalapeño pepper, seeded and finely chopped (2 teaspoons)
¾ teaspoon salt

I can usually find small red Swiss chard at my market in the spring. The ribs are quite tender in these early specimens and can be cooked successfully with the leaves. A beautiful red color, the chard is seasoned here with ginger and jalapeño pepper, with the quantity of the latter adjusted to individual tastes. If you cannot find red Swiss chard, substitute regular chard or another green, such as Romaine lettuce or watercress.

1. Trim about 2 inches from the tops of the chard leaves, and discard the trimmings. Cut the remaining chard ribs and leaves into 2-inch pieces. Wash and drain the chard. (You should have about 12 cups, lightly packed.)

2. Heat the oil in a large saucepan. When it is hot, add the shallots, and sauté them for 30 seconds over high heat. Add the ginger and jalapeño, mix well, and cook for 10 seconds.

3. Add about a third of the chard, still wet from the washing, turning it over in the pan several times to incorporate the shallots and garlic and prevent them from burning in the bottom of the pan. Then add the rest of the chard and the salt. Cover, reduce the heat to medium, and cook the mixture for 6 to 8 minutes, stirring occasionally, until the chard leaves are wilted and tender but the ribs are still slightly firm.

4. Transfer the mixture to a serving dish, and serve immediately.

YIELD: 4 SERVINGS

Nutritional analysis per serving:

Calories 137	Fat 10.4 gm.
Protein 3 gm.	Saturated fat 1.4 gm.
Carbohydrates 10 gm.	Cholesterol 0 mg.
Sodium 717 mg.	

Sautéed Lettuce Packages

3 quarts water
4 firm heads Boston lettuce
(2 pounds total)
1 tablespoon unsalted butter
1 tablespoon peanut oil
¼ teaspoon salt
⅛ teaspoon freshly ground
black pepper

Unfortunately, people don't often cook lettuce. I am very fond of it sautéed with garlic, mixed into soufflés, or combined with peas or carrots in a stew. Here, I poach whole heads of Boston lettuce, then halve them, fold them into triangle-shaped packages, and sauté them in a little butter and oil. These make a great accompaniment for Veal Chops with Olive Shavings (see page 99) or almost any roast meat. (See photograph, page 82.)

1. Bring the water to a boil in a large pot. Meanwhile, wash the lettuce thoroughly, gently opening the leaves to let water flow over and around them, but taking care not to separate the leaves from the cores.

2. Add the lettuce heads to the boiling water, and cover them with an inverted plate to keep them submerged. Bring the water back to a boil, reduce the heat to medium, and boil the lettuce gently for 20 minutes. Remove the plate, drain the water, and add enough ice to the pot to cover the lettuce and cool it quickly.

3. When the lettuce heads are cold, remove them from the pot, and, holding them gently to preserve their original shape, press each head between your palms to remove as much liquid as possible. Cut the heads in half lengthwise (top to core), then fold each half head into a triangle-shaped package. Set aside until cooking time. (The lettuce can be prepared to this point up to a day ahead, covered, and refrigerated.)

4. When you are ready to proceed, heat the butter and oil until hot in a large skillet. Add the lettuce packages, folded side up, and sprinkle them with half the salt and pepper. Cook over medium to high heat for 3 to 4 minutes. Turn the packages over, sprinkle them with the remaining salt and pepper, and sauté 3 to 4 minutes longer, until lightly browned.

YIELD: 4 SERVINGS

Nutritional analysis per serving:
Calories 96
Protein 3 gm.
Carbohydrates 8 gm.
Sodium 156 mg.
Fat 6.9 gm.
Saturated fat 2.4 gm.
Cholesterol 8 mg.

5. Arrange the lettuce packages on a serving platter, and serve immediately, two packages per person, or place them in a gratin dish, and warm them in a 180-degree oven for up to 30 minutes before serving.

SKILLET SPINACH WITH NUTMEG

1 pound spinach, trimmed of large stems and damaged leaves (about 13 ounces trimmed)
1 tablespoon unsalted butter
1 tablespoon virgin olive oil
¼ teaspoon salt
¼ teaspoon freshly ground black pepper
¼ teaspoon freshly grated nutmeg

YIELD: 4 SERVINGS

Nutritional analysis per serving:

Calories 77	Fat 6.6 gm.
Protein 3 gm.	Saturated fat 2.3 gm.
Carbohydrates 3 gm.	Cholesterol 8 mg.
Sodium 208 mg.	

The combination of nutmeg and spinach is classic in French cooking. Here, I cook freshly cleaned spinach, still wet from washing, in a little butter and oil for a minute, then season it with salt, pepper, and nutmeg, and cook it a few minutes longer to boil away excess liquid. Fast and easy, this dish is very flavorful.

1. Wash and drain the spinach. At serving time, heat the butter and oil until very hot in a large skillet. Add half the spinach (still wet from washing), and stir well. When it begins to wilt, add the remainder of the spinach to the skillet, and cover with a lid.

2. Cook the spinach for 1 minute over high heat, and then remove the lid. The spinach will be wilted, and liquid will have emerged from it. Add the salt, pepper, and nutmeg, and mix well. Continue cooking, uncovered, over high heat for 3 to 4 minutes, stirring occasionally, until most of the liquid has boiled away. Serve.

RAW RELISH OF GRAPEFRUIT AND PEACH

About ¼ red bell pepper, peeled and coarsely chopped (about 2 ounces)

1 ripe yellow peach (about 4 ounces), peeled, pitted, and coarsely chopped

1 small grapefruit (about 10 ounces), peeled, flesh segments separated from surrounding membrane, and flesh coarsely chopped (about ½ cup)

¼ cup (loose) fresh mint leaves, minced

1 small jalapeño pepper, seeded and finely chopped (about 1½ teaspoons)

2 teaspoons cider vinegar

¼ teaspoon cumin powder

⅛ teaspoon salt

1 teaspoon sugar

I enjoy relishes and try always to have some on hand. Whereas combinations that are cooked a long time will often keep for several weeks in the refrigerator, this relish—primarily a raw fruit mixture—will not last more than about a week. A fresh-tasting blend of peach and grapefruit, with a little mint and jalapeño pepper added for extra flavor, it is an ideal accompaniment for everything from game to pâtés to cold cuts to roasts, and it goes well with Venison Steaks in Sweet-Sour Sauce (recipe on page 110). (See photograph, page 84.)

1. Mix all the ingredients in a bowl. (You will have about 1½ cups.) Cover, and refrigerate for up to 1 week.

2. Serve as needed to garnish game or other meats or cold cuts.

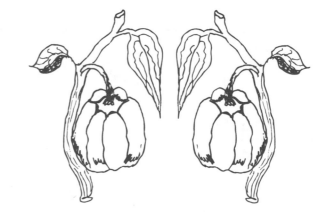

YIELD: 4 SERVINGS

Nutritional analysis per serving:

Calories 30	Fat 0.1 gm.
Protein 1 gm.	Saturated fat 0 gm.
Carbohydrates 7 gm.	Cholesterol 0 mg.
Sodium 70 mg.	

DESSERTS

SWEET APPLE FLAKE CONFECTIONS

1 firm apple (8 ounces),
  preferably Golden Delicious,
  russet, or Rome Beauty
1 pint frozen low-fat vanilla or
  coffee yogurt

 When dried in a convection oven, thin, unpeeled apple slices are transformed into crisp flakes with a flavor I find almost addictive. Pressed into scoops of frozen yogurt, as they are in this recipe, the flakes are a delicious substitute for cookies. They also make a great, healthful snack on their own and can be served as a garnish for custard or ice cream.

1. Preheat a convection oven to 250 degrees.

2. Using a sharp, thin-bladed or serrated knife, cut the unpeeled apple crosswise into slices ⅛ inch thick. You should have about sixteen slices. If desired, remove the pits from the center slices. Arrange the slices in one layer, side by side, on an aluminum cookie sheet.

3. Place the cookie sheet in the oven, and cook the apple slices for about 1 hour, until they are fairly dry and very lightly browned. Remove the slices from the sheet while they are still warm and flexible, and arrange them on a platter. Cool them to room temperature. The flakes should then be dry and crunchy. Place them in a metal or plastic storage container with a tight lid, and store at room temperature until ready to use.

4. About 1½ to 2 hours before serving time, transfer the frozen yogurt from the freezer to the refrigerator to soften.

5. At serving time, place a large scoop of frozen yogurt in the center of each of four dessert plates. Press four of the apple flakes around the sides and across the top of each scoop, encasing the scoop with the apples. (Or, arrange the apple flakes on or around the yogurt scoops in another design to your liking.) Serve immediately.

YIELD: 4 SERVINGS

Nutritional analysis per serving:

Calories 131	Fat 1.2 gm.
Protein 4 gm.	Saturated fat 0 gm.
Carbohydrates 26 gm.	Cholesterol 5 mg.
Sodium 55 mg.	

SPICY APPLE CHARLOTTE

1 tablespoon unsalted butter

1½ tablespoons corn oil or
safflower oil

2 pounds russet apples (about
5), peeled, cored, and cut into
¼-inch slices

¼ cup sugar

¼ cup honey

1 teaspoon ground cinnamon

¼ teaspoon ground allspice

⅛ teaspoon ground cloves

11 slices very thin, fine-textured
white bread (6½ ounces)

3 tablespoons strained peach
jam

1½ teaspoons Calvados (apple
brandy) (optional)

Sour cream or plain yogurt
(optional)

YIELD: 6 TO 8 SERVINGS

Nutritional analysis per serving:

Calories 260	Fat 5.8 gm.
Protein 2 gm.	Saturated fat 1.6 gm.
Carbohydrates 52 gm.	Cholesterol 5 mg.
Sodium 146 mg.	

I use russet apples here, but another variety can be substituted. The apples are cooked on top of the stove initially in a flavorful mixture of sugar, honey, and spices. Then, when most of the moisture has evaporated and the apple slices are brown, they are baked between layers of bread in a cake pan. Coat the unmolded charlotte with peach jam, and serve it in slices, warm or at room temperature, with a spoonful of sour cream or plain yogurt, if desired.

1. Preheat the oven to 375 degrees.

2. Heat the butter and 1 tablespoon of the oil in a large saucepan. When they are hot, add the apples, and sauté for 1 minute. Then add the sugar, honey, cinnamon, allspice, and cloves, mix gently, cover, and cook over medium heat for 10 minutes. Most of the moisture from the apples should be gone at this point; remove the lid, and cook the apples, uncovered, for 5 to 6 minutes, until they are nicely browned.

3. Using the remaining ½ tablespoon of oil, oil a round cake pan 8 inches in diameter and 1½ inches deep.

4. Cut 7 slices of the bread into triangles by first cutting the slices in half diagonally, then trimming the crusts from each to create smaller triangles. Lay the triangles side by side to cover the bottom of the prepared pan. Trim the remaining 4 slices of bread, cut each of them in half to make rectangles, and arrange them around the sides of the pan.

5. Spoon the apple mixture on top of the bread, and spread it evenly into the corners of the pan. Smooth the surface, and arrange the bread trimmings on top of the apples so most of them are covered.

6. Bake the charlotte at 375 degrees for 20 to 25 minutes. Meanwhile, combine the strained peach jam with the Calvados, if desired, in a small bowl.

7. Let the charlotte cool on a rack for 10 minutes, then invert it onto a plate. No more than 20 to 30 minutes before serving, coat the surface with the peach mixture (if applied earlier, the coating will be absorbed by the dessert).

8. Cut the charlotte into slices, and serve with a dollop of sour cream or yogurt, if desired.

GRATIN OF APPLES, WALNUTS, AND GRANOLA

2 apples (preferably russet or Opalescent)

1 cup low-fat granola mixture

¼ cup walnut pieces

2 tablespoons sugar

¼ cup orange juice

4 tablespoons sour cream or whipped cream for garnish (optional)

 *This recipe couldn't be easier. No need to peel the apples; just cut them into chunks, combine them with the granola, walnuts, and orange juice, press the mixture into a gratin dish, and bake. The dessert is delicious served with a little sour cream, whipped cream, or even nonfat plain yogurt.*

1. Preheat the oven to 400 degrees.

2. Cut the apples in half, core them, and cut them into 1-inch pieces. (You should have about 4 cups.)

3. Thoroughly mix the apple cubes with the remaining ingredients in a bowl, and press the mixture lightly into a 6-cup gratin dish. Bake for 1 hour, until the apples are soft and the dessert is nicely browned on top.

4. Serve lukewarm or at room temperature, topping each serving with 1 tablespoon of sour cream or whipped cream, if desired.

YIELD: 4 SERVINGS

Nutritional analysis per serving:

Calories 202	Fat 6.0 gm.
Protein 3 gm.	Saturated fat 0.5 gm.
Carbohydrates 38 gm.	Cholesterol 0 mg.
Sodium 32 mg.	

LEMON BANANAS IN CRISP SHELLS

- 2 quarts water
- 8 wonton wrappers, each about 3 inches square (2 ounces)
- 2 teaspoons canola oil
- 1½ tablespoons confectioners' sugar, plus 1 teaspoon for decoration
- 2 teaspoons grated lemon rind
- 2 tablespoons lemon juice
- ¼ cup peach preserves
- 2 tablespoons dark rum
- 2 ripe bananas (about 1 pound)

YIELD: 4 SERVINGS

Nutritional analysis per serving:

Calories 209	Fat 2.9 gm.
Protein 2 gm.	Saturated fat 0.4 gm.
Carbohydrates 42 gm.	Cholesterol 1 mg.
Sodium 92 mg.	

Instead of using rich cookie dough or puff pastry for the dessert shells here, I make them from packaged square wonton wrappers, which are fat-free. The wrappers are blanched first in boiling water, then lightly oiled, and baked until brown, crisp, and shiny on top. I create an interesting and tasty "sandwich," filling the wrappers with banana slices flavored with lemon juice and rind, dark rum, and peach preserves.

1. Preheat the oven to 375 degrees.

2. Bring the water to a boil in a pot. Drop in the wonton wrappers one at a time, and bring the water back to a boil. Boil the wrappers 1½ minutes, then drain them carefully into a colander, and return them to the pot. Fill the pot with cold water to stop the wrappers from cooking further and cool them.

3. Brush a large cookie sheet with the oil. Using both hands, carefully lift the wrappers from the cold water, shaking off as much of the water clinging to them as you can, and arrange them side by side on the oiled sheet. Place the 1½ tablespoons of confectioners' sugar in a sieve, and sprinkle it on top of the wet wonton wrappers.

4. Place the wrappers in the 375-degree oven for 16 to 18 minutes, until they are nicely browned, crisp, and glazed on the surface. Using a thin hamburger spatula, remove the hot wrappers from the cookie sheet, and place them on a rack to cool completely.

5. Mix the lemon rind, lemon juice, peach preserves, and rum in a bowl large enough to hold the bananas. Peel the bananas, and cut them in half crosswise, then into thin (1/3-inch) lengthwise slices. Add them to the bowl, and mix gently to coat the banana slices with the sauce.

6. At serving time, arrange a wonton crisp on each of four dessert plates. Divide the banana mixture among the plates, spooning it on top of the crisps. Place the remaining wonton crisps on top of the bananas, and sprinkle the remaining teaspoon of sugar on top. Serve immediately.

RED WINE AND CASSIS STRAWBERRIES

3 cups ripe strawberries, washed and hulled

3 tablespoons sugar

3 tablespoons cassis (black currant–flavored liqueur) or *crème de mûres* (blackberry–flavored liqueur)

¾ cup dry, fruity red wine

1 tablespoon shredded peppermint leaves

4 tablespoons sour cream (optional)

Cookies (optional)

YIELD: 4 SERVINGS

Nutritional analysis per serving:

Calories 133	Fat 0.4 gm.
Protein 0.1 gm.	Saturated fat 0 gm.
Carbohydrates 22 gm.	Cholesterol 0 mg.
Sodium 3 mg.	

In wine-growing regions, berries—particularly strawberries—are typically combined with the wine from that area, and sometimes a liqueur, and served as a dessert. Here, I mix strawberries with a fruity red wine and black currant or blackberry liqueur and serve them in the classic way, spooned into wine goblets. If desired, top the desserts with a little sour cream, and serve them with cookies.

1. Quarter the berries, and place them in a bowl with the sugar, liqueur, wine, and mint. Mix well, and serve immediately, or refrigerate (for up to 8 hours) until serving time.

2. Spoon the berries and marinade into wine goblets for serving. If desired, top each dessert with a dollop of sour cream, and serve it with a cookie.

SUMMER CHERRY PUDDING WITH RUM SAUCE

1½ pounds sour cherries
½ cup dry, fruity red wine
¼ cup sugar
1 10¾-ounce pound cake

RUM SAUCE
1 ripe mango (about 1 pound)
2 tablespoons honey
1 tablespoon dark rum
⅓ cup water

½ cup champagne grapes, if available, or equivalent amount of Red Flame grapes cut into ¼-inch dice, for garnish

Nutritional analysis per serving:
Calories 432
Protein 5 gm.
Carbohydrates 4 gm.
Sodium 249 mg.
Fat 12.7 gm.
Saturated fat 6.9 gm.
Cholesterol 135 mg.

This cherry pudding is a classic summer offering in England. Sour cherries are cooked briefly in wine and sugar, then layered with cake crumbs in a bowl lined with pound cake. After a few hours, the juices from the cherry mixture seep into the cake, and the dessert becomes a solid mass that takes on the shape of the bowl. Unmolded at serving time, it is presented with a sauce made from mango, honey, and rum. (See photograph, page 158.)

1. Pit the cherries, and place them in a stainless steel saucepan with the wine and sugar. Bring the mixture to a boil, uncovered, over medium heat, and cook for 5 minutes to reduce the juices. Cool. (You will have 2¼ cups.)

2. Trim the brown sides of the pound cake, reserving the trimmings. Cut the trimmed cake lengthwise into five slices, each about ½ inch thick.

3. Place a strip of parchment paper in a 4- to 6-cup bowl so that the paper covers the bottom and comes up the sides of the bowl. (This will help in the unmolding later.) Arrange three slices of the cake on top of the parchment so the cake covers the bottom and sides of the bowl.

4. Place half the cherry mixture on top of the cake and crumble half the reserved cake trimmings over the cherries. Spoon the remaining cherry mixture on top and crumble the remaining cake trimmings over it. Finish with the remaining two slices of cake, arranging them so that all the cherries are covered.

5. Cover the bowl with plastic wrap touching the cake. Place a weight of about 1 pound on top of the dessert so it presses and compacts the layers of cake and cherries. Refrigerate. (The recipe can be prepared to this point up to 2 days ahead.)

FOR THE RUM SAUCE

6. Peel the mango, and cut the flesh from the pit. Place the flesh in a food processor or blender with the honey, rum, and water, and process until smooth. (You will have 1¾ cups.)

7. When ready to serve, unmold the cake onto a serving plate, pour the mango sauce around it, and sprinkle with the grapes. Spoon onto dessert dishes at the table.

MANGO SYMPHONY

1 ripe mango (about 1 pound)
2 Santa Rosa or Black Friar plums (8 ounces)
3 tablespoons honey
2 tablespoons dark rum of best quality

After marinating in a honey-rum sauce, pieces of plum are spooned into the center of plates ringed with mango slices, and the remaining sauce is drizzled over both fruits. The result is a wonderfully complementary blend of flavors.

1. Peel the mango, and slice it thinly, cutting all around the central pit and discarding it. Place the slices in a bowl, cover, and refrigerate until cold.

2. Halve the plums, discard the pits, and cut the flesh into ½-inch pieces. (You should have about 2 cups.) Mix the honey and rum in a bowl large enough to hold the plums. Add the plum pieces, mix well, cover, and refrigerate until cold.

3. At serving time, arrange the slices of mango around the periphery of four dessert plates. Spoon the plums into the center of the plates and drizzle the remaining marinade from the plums over all the fruit. Serve immediately.

YIELD: 4 SERVINGS

Nutritional analysis per serving:

Calories 145	Fat 0.5 gm.
Protein 0.1 gm.	Saturated fat 0.1 gm.
Carbohydrates 33 gm.	Cholesterol 0 mg.
Sodium 2 mg.	

PEARS IN GRENADINE

6 medium Bosc pears
(2 pounds)
⅓ cup lime juice
⅓ cup sugar
⅓ cup grenadine
1 cup dry white wine
1 cup water

YIELD: 4 SERVINGS

Nutritional analysis per serving:
Calories 220
Protein 1 gm.
Carbohydrates 49 gm.
Sodium 5 mg.
Fat 0.7 gm.
Saturated fat 0 gm.
Cholesterol 0 mg.

 The time required to cook pears varies dramatically, and this must be taken into account when preparing this and other recipes. I use firm Bosc pears here, peeling and coring them before cooking, and even though the cooking liquids boil up inside the pears in this preparation, it takes them 30 minutes to get tender. Well-ripened Anjou or Bartlett pears, on the other hand, cook in as little as 2 or 3 minutes, while Seckels can take as long as 1 hour.

Folded paper towels are placed on top of the pears in the pan to absorb some of the surrounding liquid and keep the pear tops moist, thus preventing them from discoloring as they cook. When cooked, the pears—saturated with the cooking juices—sink into the liquid. (See photograph, page 124.)

1. Peel and core the pears, leaving the stems attached and a little of the skin in place around the stems for decoration. Stand the pears upright in a saucepan that will hold them snugly in one layer, and add the lime juice, sugar, grenadine, white wine, and water. (The liquid should barely cover the pears.) Fold a length of paper towel in half and then in half again, and place it over the pears to cover their tops completely.

2. Bring the liquid to a boil over medium to high heat, then reduce the heat to low, cover, and boil the pears gently for about 30 minutes, or until they are very tender when pierced with the point of a sharp knife.

3. Set the pears off the heat, and let them cool in the pan for about 15 minutes, then lift them from the pan, and stand them upright in a serving dish. There should be about 2½ cups of cooking liquid remaining. Return the pan to the stove, and boil the liquid over high heat until it is reduced to a syrup. (You will have 1 cup.)

4. Pour the syrup over the pears, cover, and refrigerate until cold. Serve one pear per person with some of the surrounding syrup.

BROILED FIGS IN PEACH SAUCE

1 pound ripe black figs (often called Mission figs)

1½ tablespoons sugar

PEACH SAUCE

¼ cup peach preserves

2 tablespoons lemon juice

2 tablespoons dark rum

Wait to do this dessert until ripe figs are available. As in most fruit desserts, the ripeness of the fruit determines the quality of the dish. The figs are halved, sprinkled with sugar, then broiled to caramelize their tops. They are served with a mixture of peach preserves, lemon juice, and rum. (See photograph, page 124.)

1. Preheat a broiler.

2. Cut the figs in half lengthwise, and arrange them cut side up in one layer in a gratin dish. Sprinkle with the sugar.

3. Place the figs under the broiler about 3 inches from the heat for 5 to 6 minutes, until they are slightly caramelized on top and are soft when pierced with the tines of a fork. Set aside to cool while you make the peach sauce.

FOR THE PEACH SAUCE

4. In a small bowl, mix the peach preserves, lemon juice, and rum.

5. Spoon the sauce over the figs, and let them rest at room temperature until serving time. Serve at room temperature.

YIELD: 4 SERVINGS

Nutritional analysis per serving:

Calories 168	Fat 0.4 gm.
Protein 1 gm.	Saturated fat 0.1 gm.
Carbohydrates 40 gm.	Cholesterol 0 mg.
Sodium 11 mg.	

Grapefruit in Nectar

2 pink grapefruit (2 pounds)
1½ cups cold water for blanching, plus 2 tablespoons water for the caramel
¼ cup sugar
1 tablespoon grenadine syrup
1 tablespoon Cointreau or other liqueur to your liking

For best results, use large, flavorful pink grapefruit for this recipe. Wedgelike pieces of grapefruit flesh are removed from their surrounding membranes and served in a sauce composed of the juice squeezed from the membranes, a caramel made of sugar and water, and—for added flavor—grenadine and Cointreau.

1. Using a vegetable peeler, remove six strips of grapefruit peel from areas where the skin color is brightest. Stack the strips together and cut them lengthwise into long, thin julienne strips. (You should have about ¼ cup.) Place the julienne in a small, high-sided saucepan, cover it with the 1½ cups of water, and bring to a boil. Boil for 12 to 20 seconds, then drain and rinse the julienne in a sieve held under cold, running water. Drain well, and set the julienne aside in a small bowl.

2. Using a sharp knife, peel the grapefruit, removing and discarding all the remaining skin and cottony pith, so the flesh of the fruit is totally exposed. Then cut between the membranes on each side of the grapefruit segments, and remove the flesh in wedgelike pieces. You should have ten to twelve segments per grapefruit. Place these in a bowl, and sprinkle the blanched julienne on top. Squeeze the membranes through a sieve set over a bowl, pressing them to remove as much juice as possible. Reserve this juice. (You should have ⅓ to ½ cup.)

3. Place the sugar and the 2 tablespoons of water in a small saucepan, bring the mixture to a full boil, and boil it over high heat for about 3 minutes, until it becomes a dark blond caramel. Remove the pan from the heat, and carefully add 1 or 2 tablespoons of the reserved grapefruit juice, taking care to avoid splatters from the hot caramel. Shake the pan to mix in the juice. Add the rest of the juice, and mix well with a whisk until the juice is incorporated.

4. Pour the caramel sauce over the grapefruit segments in the bowl, and mix well. Add the grenadine and Cointreau,

YIELD: 4 SERVINGS

Nutritional analysis per serving:

Calories 100	Fat 0.1 gm.
Protein 1 gm.	Saturated fat 0 gm.
Carbohydrates 24 gm.	Cholesterol 0 mg.
Sodium 0 mg.	

and mix again. Cover, and refrigerate until serving time. The recipe can be prepared to this point up to 8 hours ahead.

5. To serve, lift the grapefruit segments from the bowl with a slotted spoon, and divide them among four dessert plates. Pour the juices over and around them, and serve.

APRICOT *DÉLICE*

½ **cup apricot or peach preserves**

1 **cup Sauternes (sweet wine)**

1 **stalk fresh basil**

2 **tablespoons water**

8 **ripe apricots (1¼ pounds), washed**

1 **kiwi (about 3 ounces)**

8 **fresh basil leaves, for decoration**

Délice is the French word for "delight," which accurately describes this fruit dessert. Fresh apricots are cooked in a sweet wine that is flavored with basil, and then cooled. With the addition of diced kiwi, the cooking liquid is transformed into a sauce and spooned over the apricots at serving time. (See photograph, page 124.)

1. Place the apricot preserves, Sauternes, basil stalk, and water in a saucepan measuring about 7 inches across (just large enough to hold the apricots snugly in one layer). Bring the mixture to a boil, and add the apricots. (They should be barely covered with the liquid.) Bring back to a boil, cover, and boil the apricots gently for 5 minutes, or until they are just tender. Let cool, covered, in the liquid.

2. Meanwhile, peel the kiwi, and cut the flesh into ¼-inch dice.

3. At serving time, arrange two apricots on each plate. Discard the basil stalk, and toss the kiwi pieces in the cooking juice. Coat the apricots with the juice, and divide the remaining juice and kiwi pieces among the four plates. Decorate each apricot with a basil leaf, and serve.

YIELD: 4 SERVINGS

Nutritional analysis per serving:

Calories 211	Fat 0.7 gm.
Protein 2 gm.	Saturated fat 0 gm.
Carbohydrates 44 gm.	Cholesterol 0 mg.
Sodium 21 mg.	

PINEAPPLE IN CANTALOUPE SAUCE

About ½ of a ripe cantaloupe
    (1 pound)
3 tablespoons honey
2 tablespoons Grand Marnier
About ⅓ of a ripe pineapple
    (1 pound)
2 red Santa Rosa plums (about
    6 ounces total)

Three fruits are represented here: pineapple and plum slices are served in a beautiful sauce created by processing the flesh of cantaloupe. This dish is best if made with only ripe, full-flavored fruit. The cantaloupe sauce can be used as a marinade for other fruit if ripe pineapple and plums are not available. Good substitutes would be watermelon, honeydew melon, or apples.

1. Remove the rind and seeds from the cantaloupe, and cut the flesh into 1-inch pieces. You should have about 2 cups. Place the pieces in the bowl of a food processor with the honey, and process until smooth. Pour the puree into a bowl, and stir in the Grand Marnier. Cover, and refrigerate until ready to serve. (You should have about 1½ cups.)

2. Remove the rind and core from the pineapple, and cut the flesh crosswise into ⅛-inch-thick slices. You should have about twenty slices.

3. Cut the plums in half crosswise, remove the pits, and cut the flesh into slices ⅛ inch thick. You should have about twenty slices.

4. At serving time, divide the cantaloupe sauce among four dessert plates. Arrange four or five slices of pineapple on top of the sauce on each plate, and place a plum slice on top of the pineapple. Arrange the remaining plum slices around the periphery of each plate to create a decorative border. Serve.

YIELD: 4 SERVINGS

Nutritional analysis per serving:

Calories 470	Fat 4.4 gm.
Protein 6 gm.	Saturated fat 0.3 gm.
Carbohydrates 111 gm.	Cholesterol 0 mg.
Sodium 6 mg.	

BLACKBERRIES IN CREAMY HONEY SAUCE

- 2 cups (1 pint) blackberries
- 1 tablespoon sugar
- 3 tablespoons honey
- ¼ cup orange juice
- 1 cup nonfat plain yogurt
- 1 tablespoon shredded fresh peppermint leaves

For this dessert, ripe blackberries are tossed in a little sugar and mounded on plates coated with a sauce composed of honey, orange juice, yogurt, and mint. Quick and easy, the dish is as attractive as it is flavorful. Any other berries—strawberries, raspberries, boysenberries—can be substituted here. Be sure to choose very ripe berries for maximum sweetness.

1. Gently toss the blackberries and sugar in a small bowl. Cover, and refrigerate until serving time.

2. Meanwhile, mix the honey and orange juice in another small bowl. When the mixture is smooth, add the yogurt and mint, and mix just until smooth. Cover, and refrigerate until serving time.

3. To serve, divide the yogurt sauce among four dessert plates. Mound some berries in the center, dividing them equally among the plates. Serve immediately.

YIELD: 4 SERVINGS

Nutritional analysis per serving:

Calories 137	Fat 0.4 gm.
Protein 4 gm.	Saturated fat 0.1 gm.
Carbohydrates 31 gm.	Cholesterol 1 mg.
Sodium 44 mg.	

Raspberry Trifle with Nectarine Sauce

1 pint nonfat plain yogurt
4 ounces pound cake, homemade or store-bought
¼ cup coffee extract (the first ¼ cup from a pot of drip coffee)
8 ounces fresh raspberries

NECTARINE SAUCE

⅓ cup peach preserves
3 tablespoons orange juice
1 nectarine (8 ounces), pitted and cut into ¼-inch pieces (1 cup)
1 tablespoon cognac

4 small sprigs mint, for decoration

Fresh raspberries are the centerpiece of this trifle, which also includes pound cake moistened and flavored with a little coffee extract. I use homemade yogurt cheese in place of the fresh cream traditionally found in this classic dessert, thus dropping the calorie count substantially. The cheese is made by placing nonfat plain yogurt in a strainer and draining it for at least 12 hours to remove the liquid whey.

When considering the use of nonfat yogurt as an alternative ingredient in recipes, compare the following figures: 1 cup of nonfat yogurt contains 120 calories; 1 cup of sour cream contains 490 calories; 1 cup of heavy cream contains 830 calories; and 1 cup of mayonnaise contains 1580 calories.

1. Place the yogurt in a strainer lined with paper towels, set over a bowl. Cover the yogurt with plastic wrap, and refrigerate it for at least 12 hours and as long as 24. There will be about 1 cup of liquid whey in the bowl, which can be drunk or discarded, and about 1 cup (8 ounces) of yogurt cheese in the strainer. Set aside 6 tablespoons (4½ ounces) of the cheese for use in this recipe. Reserve the remainder of the cheese for another use.

2. Cut the pound cake into eight slices, each about ⅜ inch thick. Then cut the slices into rounds 2½ to 2¾ inches in diameter with a cookie cutter. Reserve the cake trimmings. Place a cake round in the bottom of each of four small (½-cup) soufflé molds about 2¾ inches in diameter.

3. Using a brush or teaspoon, moisten each round of cake with about 1 teaspoon of the coffee extract. Place about ¾ tablespoon of yogurt cheese on top of each round, and press about 8 raspberries into the cheese. Coarsely crumble some of the reserved cake trimmings on top of the cheese, and moisten the trimmings with about 1 teaspoon of the remaining coffee extract. Place another ¾ tablespoon of cheese on top of the crumbs, and press another 8 raspberries into the cheese. Top each dessert with another cake round, moisten the rounds with the remaining coffee extract, and press them into place. Cover tightly with plastic wrap, and refrigerate. (The desserts can be prepared to this point up to 8 hours ahead.)

FOR THE NECTARINE SAUCE

4. Place the preserves, orange juice, nectarine pieces, and cognac in a bowl. Mix well, cover, and refrigerate.

5. At serving time, run a knife around the inside edge of the soufflé molds, and unmold the trifles onto dessert plates. Coat with the nectarine sauce and decorate each serving with a sprig of mint.

YIELD: 4 SERVINGS

Nutritional analysis per serving:

Calories 257	Fat 6.2 gm.
Protein 4 gm.	Saturated fat 3.2 gm.
Carbohydrates 46 gm.	Cholesterol 63 mg.
Sodium 139 mg.	

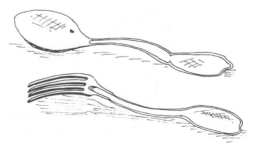

CRANBERRY SOUFFLÉS WITH CRANBERRY— RED WINE SAUCE

1 tablespoon unsalted butter (to butter the molds)
1 10-ounce package fresh cranberries
⅓ cup sugar
½ cup apricot or peach jam
¼ cup water
¾ cup fruity, dry red wine
3 egg whites
Confectioners' sugar, for sprinkling on the finished soufflés

Fresh cranberries, available much of the year now at most supermarkets, are used in this dessert. The berries are cooked first with a little sugar and jam, then some of the mixture is pureed and combined with wine to create a flavorful sauce, and the remainder is folded into egg whites for the soufflé. Small, disposable aluminum molds can be used here, or the soufflés can be baked in conventional glass, ceramic, or metal molds.

The assembled soufflés can be cooked immediately, of course, but they can also be refrigerated for a few hours, or even frozen, before cooking. If you decide to make them ahead and freeze them, transfer the frozen molds directly from the freezer to the hot oven, and cook the soufflés as indicated in the recipe. (See photograph, page 159.)

1. If you will bake the soufflés immediately after preparing them, preheat the oven to 375 degrees.

2. Butter four ¾-cup aluminum, ovenproof glass, or ceramic molds. Set them aside.

3. Combine the cranberries, sugar, jam, and water in a large stainless steel saucepan, and bring the mixture to a boil over medium to high heat. Cover the saucepan, reduce the heat to very low, and cook gently for 20 minutes. (You will have about 1¾ cups.)

4. Place ¾ cup of the cranberry mixture in the bowl of a food processor, and process it until smooth. Add the red wine, process briefly, and strain the mixture through a fine strainer set over a bowl. Set the sauce aside until serving time.

5. Beat the egg whites until they are firm. Working as quickly as you can, fold them into the remaining cup of cooked cranberries. Fill the prepared molds with the mixture, and either bake immediately, or cover and refrigerate the molds for up to 2 hours before baking, or cover and freeze them for up to 2 weeks before baking.

6. If you are baking the soufflés immediately or after a brief refrigeration, arrange the filled molds on an aluminum tray, and place them in the 375-degree oven for 13 to 15 minutes, until they are puffy on top and set in the center. If you are baking frozen soufflés, place them on a tray directly from the freezer, and bake in a preheated 375-degree oven for 15 to 18 minutes. (If the soufflés begin to darken on top after 10 to 12 minutes, place a sheet of aluminum foil loosely on top of them for the remainder of the cooking period.) When they are done, sprinkle the hot soufflés with the confectioners' sugar.

7. To serve the soufflés, divide the sauce among four plates. Using a large spoon, scoop the soufflés from the molds, and place one in the center of each plate. Serve immediately.

YIELD: 4 SERVINGS

Nutritional analysis per serving:

Calories 265	Fat 3.1 gm.
Protein 3 gm.	Saturated fat 1.8 gm.
Carbohydrates 52 gm.	Cholesterol 8 mg.
Sodium 61 mg.	

RASPBERRY VELVET

1 package (12 ounces) IQF (individually quick frozen) unsweetened raspberries, defrosted, or an equivalent amount of fresh raspberries (about 12 ounces)

¼ cup water

⅓ cup seedless black raspberry preserves

2 teaspoons lime juice

1 tablespoon sugar

4 sprigs fresh mint

 I often use individually quick frozen (IQF) berries. Available year round at most supermarkets, they are generally berries of high quality that have been picked and frozen (without sugar) at the peak of ripeness. Of course, if you have access to fresh raspberries, by all means use them.

The berries are liquefied and strained here first, then the mixture is partially frozen and, finally, the slush is served in sugar-rimmed glasses. If you prepare the dessert ahead and freeze the mixture until hard, be sure to defrost it under refrigeration for an hour or so before serving, to achieve the desired slushy consistency.

1. Push the raspberries through a food mill with the black raspberry preserves, then strain the mixture through a fine-mesh strainer set over a bowl to eliminate any remaining seeds. Add the water, and mix well. (You will have about 2 cups.)

2. Place the bowl containing the berry mixture in the freezer, and stir it occasionally until it is half frozen and slushy in consistency.

3. Meanwhile, place the lime juice in one small saucer and the sugar in another. Dip the rims of four stemmed glasses (preferably tulip champagne glasses) first into the lime juice and then into the sugar, to create a border. Place the glasses in the freezer or refrigerator until serving time.

4. At serving time, divide the raspberry velvet among the prepared glasses, and decorate each with a sprig of mint. Serve immediately.

YIELD: 4 SERVINGS

Nutritional analysis per serving:
Calories 124   Fat 0.9 gm.
Protein 1 gm.   Saturated fat 0 gm.
Carbohydrates 32 gm.   Cholesterol 0 mg.
Sodium 11 mg.

TARTELETTES AUX FRUITS PANACHÉS (SEE PAGE 176).

SUMMER CHERRY PUDDING WITH RUM SAUCE (SEE PAGE 144).

CLOCKWISE FROM TOP: CARAMEL CUPS WITH COFFEE FROZEN YOGURT (SEE PAGE 172) AND CRYSTALLIZED ROSE PETALS (SEE PAGE 161); ICE-CREAM PHYLLO NAPOLEONS (SEE PAGE 169); CRANBERRY SOUFFLÉS WITH CRANBERRY-RED WINE SAUCE (SEE PAGE 154).

FARINA BAVARIAN CREAM CAKE WITH APRICOT SAUCE (SEE PAGE 166).

160

CRYSTALLIZED MINT LEAVES AND ROSE PETALS

About ⅓ of 1 egg white

⅓   **cup sugar**

12   **large fresh mint leaves, cleaned and dried, or 12 pink or red rose petals**

Many desserts can be enhanced by the addition of these crystallized mint leaves and rose petals, both of which lend eye appeal and flavor. Basil leaves can be handled in the same manner with equally good results. The clean leaves and petals are dipped in lightly beaten egg whites first, then in granulated sugar. When the sugar dries, it crystallizes, forming a sugar coating on the leaves and petals, and they can be kept for at least a week in a tightly closed container. They provide a special decorative touch to cakes, ice cream (see Caramel Cups with Coffee Frozen Yogurt, page 172), or custard. (See photograph, page 159.)

1. In a bowl, beat the egg white lightly with a fork to loosen and liquefy it. Spread the sugar on a cookie sheet. Line another cookie sheet with plastic wrap.

2. Dip the mint leaves or the rose petals one at a time in the egg white, and then run your finger lightly over both sides to remove most of the white. (The leaves or petals should be wet but not heavily coated with the egg white.) Lay each leaf or petal flat in the sugar and sprinkle some of the surrounding sugar on top. Press firmly with your fingers so the sugar covers the surface totally and adheres.

3. Transfer the coated leaves or petals to the cookie sheet lined with plastic, and set them aside to dry at room temperature. Discard any leftover egg white and sugar. When the sugar has dried and crystallized on the leaves or petals, store them at room temperature in a metal or plastic container with a tight lid. They will keep for up to a week.

YIELD: 4 SERVINGS OF EITHER

Nutritional analysis per serving:

Calories 50	Fat 0 gm.
Protein 0.3 gm.	Saturated fat 0 gm.
Carbohydrates 13 gm.	Cholesterol 0 mg.
Sodium 4 mg.	

SOUFFLÉ OF MANGO WITH MANGO SAUCE

1 teaspoon unsalted butter

4 tablespoons granulated sugar

2 very ripe mangoes (about
   1 pound each)

2 tablespoons grenadine syrup

2 tablespoons Grand Marnier

2 tablespoons water

3 egg whites

1 teaspoon confectioners' sugar

2 kiwis (about 3 ounces each),
   peeled and cut into ½-inch
   dice (⅔ cup)

The flesh of two ripe mangoes is pureed here, with half the puree strained to make a sauce and the remainder combined with beaten egg whites for the soufflé. Because there are no egg yolks in the base of this souf-flé—it consists solely of mango puree and a little sugar—the assembled dish will keep, refrigerated, for a few hours before baking, provided the egg whites are well beaten and stiff. In fact, the unbaked soufflé can even be frozen for up to 2 weeks. Place it in the freezer uncovered until firm (so the covering material won't stick to its exposed surface), then cover it for the remainder of its time in the freezer. When you are ready to cook the soufflé, let it defrost partially, uncovered, at room temperature for an hour or so before baking it.

1. If you will bake the soufflé immediately after preparing it, preheat the oven to 375 degrees.

2. Using the butter and 1 tablespoon of the granulated sugar, butter and sugar a 3½-to-4-cup soufflé mold.

3. Peel and pit the mangoes, and puree the flesh in a food processor. (You should have 2 cups.) Set 1 cup of the puree aside in a bowl large enough to hold the soufflé mixture. Strain the remaining cup of puree through a fine strainer set over a small bowl. (You should have about ¾ cup strained.)

4. Add the grenadine, Grand Marnier, and water to the strained puree, cover, and refrigerate. (You should have about 1¼ cups of mango sauce.)

5. Beat the egg whites by hand or with a mixer until stiff, then add the remaining 3 tablespoons of granulated sugar, and beat a few more seconds. Add about half of the beaten whites to the reserved cup of mango puree, and mix with a whisk. Then, working as quickly as you can, gently but thoroughly fold in the rest of the egg whites with a rubber spatula.

6. Fill the prepared mold with the soufflé mixture. Smooth the top, then decorate it with ridges or lines, if desired, using the blade of a knife or metal spatula.

7. If baking the soufflé immediately, place it in the 375-degree oven for about 25 minutes, until it is puffed and golden on top. Alternatively, refrigerate the soufflé, uncovered, for up to an hour, and then bake it; or freeze it, uncovered, for at least 12 hours until solid, then cover it with plastic wrap (which won't stick to the frozen soufflé), and freeze for up to 2 weeks. Remove the soufflé from the freezer 1 hour before baking, immediately peel off the plastic wrap, and let the soufflé sit at room temperature to partially defrost, while you preheat the oven to 350 degrees. Bake the soufflé for 35 to 40 minutes, until it is puffed, golden, and set.

8. Sprinkle the hot soufflé with the confectioners' sugar. Divide the sauce among four dessert plates, and sprinkle the diced kiwi on top. Bring the soufflé to the table, and serve large spoonfuls of it on top of the sauce.

YIELD: 4 SERVINGS

Nutritional analysis per serving:

Calories 233	Fat 1.5 gm.
Protein 4 gm.	Saturated fat 0.7 gm.
Carbohydrates 52 gm.	Cholesterol 3 mg.
Sodium 46 mg.	

Oeufs à la Neige in Peach Sauce

PEACH SAUCE

- ¾ cup nonfat plain yogurt
- ¾ cup sliced peaches in syrup
- 1½ tablespoons sugar
- 1½ tablespoons Cointreau or Grand Marnier
- ½ teaspoon vanilla extract

SNOW EGGS

- 6 cups water
- 3 large egg whites
- ¼ cup sugar

CARAMEL

- 3 tablespoons sugar
- 1 tablespoon water

ANGEL HAIR
(ALTERNATIVE TOPPING)

- 1 cup sugar
- ¼ cup water
- 2 teaspoons grated edible wax, such as beeswax

A classic French dessert, oeufs à la neige, or snow eggs, consists of egg-shaped portions of meringue dropped into hot water and cooked briefly on top of the stove. I serve the snow eggs with a sauce made of canned peaches pureed with yogurt, a little sugar, Cointreau, and vanilla. Although similar in color and consistency to crème anglaise, the rich custard sauce traditionally served with the "eggs," it is much less caloric.

The snow eggs may be finished in the conventional manner, with a drizzle of caramel on top, or with caramel angel hair. For the angel hair, I add a little beeswax to a hot caramel (a trick I learned from my good friend and fellow chef Jean-Claude Szurdak). The wax coats the sugar threads, making them less likely to stick together. Protect the angel hair from any humidity.

FOR THE PEACH SAUCE

1. Place the yogurt, peaches (with syrup), 1½ tablespoons sugar, Cointreau, and vanilla in a blender or food processor, and process until smooth and foamy. If desired, strain the peach sauce through a fine-mesh strainer set over a bowl.

FOR THE SNOW EGGS

2. Bring the water to a boil in a large pot. Meanwhile, beat the egg whites in a mixer until they are firm (3 to 4 minutes). Add the ¼ cup sugar, and continue beating the whites at medium to high speed for 30 seconds. At this point, reduce the heat of the water so that it is no more than 180 degrees (just under the simmer/boil).

3. Using a ladle or a large spoon, scoop out four mounds of meringue one at a time, and, using another spoon, slide them into the hot (not boiling) water. Poach the egg white mounds for about 2½ minutes, then use a skimmer to gently turn them over, and cook for another 2½ minutes. Lift them carefully from the water, and drain them on paper towels.

FOR THE CARAMEL

4. Not more than 3 hours before serving the snow eggs, place the 3 tablespoons of sugar and 1 tablespoon of water in a small, unlined copper or stainless steel saucepan. Mix just enough to combine them, then bring to a boil over high heat. Reduce the heat to medium, and continue boiling the mixture for about 3 minutes, until it thickens into a syrup and turns a rich caramel color, taking care that it doesn't burn.

5. While the caramel is cooking, pour the peach sauce into a serving dish or shallow glass bowl and arrange the snow eggs on top in one layer. Remove the caramel from the stove, and immediately pour it directly on top of the "eggs," dividing it equally among them. Serve, preferably within an hour.

FOR THE ANGEL HAIR (ALTERNATIVE TOPPING)

6. Combine the sugar and water in a small saucepan, bring to a boil over medium heat, and cook until a light ivory in color (about 335 degrees). Remove from the heat, and stir in the wax.

7. Cover the floor surrounding your work table with newspapers, and secure a long-handled spatula or wooden spoon so that the entire handle extends beyond the edge of the table.

8. When the syrup has cooled for a few minutes, hold two forks side by side in one hand (or use a small whisk with the wires clipped off where they begin to curve), and dip the tines into the pan. Lift some syrup, and wave the forks high over the spatula so that the dripping threads solidify in the air before falling over the extended handle.

9. Slide the collected strands off the handle, and use immediately to garnish the "eggs" or store in an airtight container.

YIELD: 4 SERVINGS

Nutritional analysis per serving with caramel topping:

Calories 192	Fat 0.1 gm.
Protein 5 gm.	Saturated fat 0.1 gm.
Carbohydrates 41 gm.	Cholesterol 1 mg.
Sodium 77 mg.	

FARINA BAVARIAN CREAM CAKE WITH APRICOT SAUCE

CAKE

2½ cups nonfat milk
Grated rind of 1 orange
      (1½ teaspoons)
Grated rind of 1 lemon
      (1 teaspoon)
  1 teaspoon pure vanilla extract
  ¼ cup farina (Cream of Wheat)
  1 envelope plain gelatin
      (2 teaspoons)
  ⅓ cup sugar
  ½ cup heavy cream
  ¼ teaspoon canola oil

APRICOT SAUCE

  ¾ cup (about 8 ounces) apricot
      preserves
  2 tablespoons lemon juice
  2 tablespoons cognac
  2 teaspoons julienned lemon
      peel
  1 to 2 tablespoons water
      (optional)

Farina is probably better known in the United States as Cream of Wheat and is sold here under that name, but in France and elsewhere in the world this word means plain white flour, which obviously would not work in this recipe. I cook a small amount of American-style farina in nonfat milk for this lighter version of the classic Bavarian cream cake, traditionally made with whole milk and egg yolks and finished with lots of heavy cream.

For this dessert serving six to eight people, I use only ½ cup (8 tablespoons) of cream. Since cream doubles in volume when whipped, this will yield 1 cup of whipped cream. The calories by volume are cut in half as well: whereas 1 tablespoon of heavy cream contains 40 calories, 1 tablespoon of whipped cream has only 20 calories, about as many as a like amount of sour cream.

Served with apricot preserves flavored with lemon juice and cognac, this is an ideal party dessert. You may decorate the cake, if you wish, with apricot preserves and a little melted chocolate. (See photograph, page 160.)

FOR THE CAKE

1. Combine the milk, orange rind, lemon rind, and vanilla in a large saucepan, and bring the mixture to a boil over medium to high heat. Meanwhile, in a small bowl mix together the farina, gelatin, and sugar. When the milk comes to a boil, stir in the farina mixture, and bring back to a boil. Reduce the heat to low, and boil gently, stirring occasionally, for 4 to 5 minutes. Then remove from the heat, and set aside to cool to lukewarm in the pan.

2. Meanwhile, pour the cream into a small mixing bowl, and beat it until firm. (You should have about 1 cup, whipped.) Add the cream to the lukewarm farina mixture, and fold it in gently but thoroughly.

DECORATION (OPTIONAL)

3 tablespoons apricot
   preserves, strained

Red, green, and yellow food
   coloring

1 tablespoon melted bittersweet
   or semisweet chocolate

YIELD: 4 SERVINGS

Nutritional analysis per serving:

Calories 247	Fat 6.7 gm.
Protein 5 gm.	Saturated fat 4.0 gm.
Carbohydrates 41 gm.	Cholesterol 25 mg.
Sodium 68 mg.	

3. Oil a round cake pan 8 inches in diameter and 1½ inches deep with the canola oil, and line the bottom with parchment paper, to make unmolding the cake easier. (You can also lay a 1-inch strip of parchment paper across the bottom of the pan with both ends extending about 1 inch beyond the rim on opposite sides; pulling gently on these ends will help lift the cake and release it from the pan.) Pour the cake mixture into the pan, smooth the top, cover with plastic wrap, and refrigerate for at least 2 hours and as long as 48 hours.

FOR THE APRICOT SAUCE

4. Mix the preserves, lemon juice, cognac, and julienned peel together in a small bowl. If a thinner sauce is desired, add the water as necessary.

5. To serve, unmold the cake upside down, cut it into wedges, and place on dessert plates, spooning about 2 tablespoons of apricot sauce over each serving.

FOR DECORATING THE CAKE (OPTIONAL)

6. Make four small cornets of parchment or wax paper.

7. Place 1 tablespoon of strained apricot preserves in each of three small dishes. Add one or two drops of red food coloring to one, green food coloring to the second, and yellow to the third.

8. Pour the melted chocolate into one of the cornets, and cut off the tip of the cornet. Create a freehand design on the surface of the unmolded cake, drawing with the chocolate to make long stems, flower outlines, and/or ivy leaves.

9. Spoon a different colored preserve into each of the remaining cornets, and cut off the tips. Gently press the preserves into the chocolate outlines, filling in the leaves and flowers to create a stained-glass-window effect.

CREAMY RICE PUDDING WITH FRUIT SAUCE

RICE PUDDING

- ⅓ cup (about 3 ounces) sweet Japanese-type white rice or another white rice variety
- ½ teaspoon cinnamon
- 3 cups nonfat milk, plus a few tablespoons, if needed
- 2 tablespoons pure maple syrup
- ½ teaspoon pure vanilla extract

FRUIT SAUCE

- ½ cup sweet apple cider, less 1 tablespoon to mix with cornstarch (see below)
- ½ cup fruity red wine
- 2 tablespoons honey
- 1 cup (about 5 ounces) seedless red grapes
- 1 red plum (about 4 ounces), cut into ½-inch pieces (½ cup)
- 1 teaspoon cornstarch dissolved in 1 tablespoon cider (see above)
- 1 kiwi (about 4 ounces), peeled and cut into ½-inch dice (⅓ cup)

YIELD: 4 SERVINGS

Nutritional analysis per serving:

Calories 245	Fat 0.8 gm.
Protein 7 gm.	Saturated fat 0.3 gm.
Carbohydrates 45 gm.	Cholesterol 4 mg.
Sodium 103 mg.	

I prefer this recipe prepared with a sweet Japanese-type rice, but another white rice can be used as well. A very small amount of rice—only ⅓ cup—is cooked in 3 cups of nonfat milk for a long time, and the resulting mixture is almost a puree.

FOR THE RICE PUDDING

1. Preheat the oven to 350 degrees.

2. Combine the rice and cinnamon in a large ovenproof saucepan. Stir in the 3 cups milk, and bring the mixture to a boil over medium to high heat, stirring occasionally to prevent the milk from scorching. Cover the pan, and place it in the oven for 40 minutes.

3. Remove the rice from the oven. The mixture will be very mushy at this point, with a lot of liquid around the rice. Add the maple syrup and vanilla, and mix them in lightly. Transfer the mixture to a bowl, and set it aside, covered, to cool. When cool, refrigerate.

FOR THE FRUIT SAUCE

4. Place the cider and wine in a clean saucepan, and bring the mixture to a boil over high heat. Add the honey, grapes, and plum, and return the mixture to a boil. Cover the pan, reduce the heat to low, and boil gently for 5 minutes. Mix in the dissolved cornstarch, and remove the pan from the heat. Add the kiwi, and pour the sauce into a bowl. Cool completely, cover, and refrigerate.

5. Although the rice mixture will thicken in the refrigerator, it should still be soft. At serving time, if it has thickened so much that it mounds on a spoon, stir in a little milk to thin it. Divide the cold pudding among four soup plates, and ladle the fruit sauce on top.

ICE-CREAM PHYLLO NAPOLEONS

2 teaspoons unsalted butter, melted

2 teaspoons canola oil

2 phyllo leaves, 14 inches by 18 inches (about 1½ ounces)

2½ tablespoons confectioners' sugar, plus 1½ teaspoons for decoration (optional)

1 pint Rocky Road low-calorie ice cream (10 to 12 ounces) or another low-calorie flavor to your liking

Prepared in the style of a classic napoleon, which is traditionally made with puff pastry, this dessert uses packaged phyllo leaves, a much lighter alternative. I brush two of the thin pastry leaves with a little butter, oil, and sugar, cut them into squares, and bake them. Low-calorie ice cream is sandwiched between the squares, and the stacked desserts are sprinkled with a little confectioners' sugar before serving. (See photograph, page 159.)

1. Preheat the oven to 400 degrees.

2. Mix the melted butter and oil together in a small bowl. Spread one of the phyllo leaves on a cookie sheet, and brush it with the butter and oil mixture. Place the tablespoons of confectioners' sugar in a sieve, and sprinkle about half of it evenly over the phyllo leaf. Place the second phyllo leaf on top, aligning it with the first, and repeat the buttering and sugaring procedure, using the rest of the butter-oil mixture and sugar in the sieve.

3. With a large, sharp knife, cut the stacked phyllo leaves into twelve equal squares, four running the length of the rectangle and three across the width. Bake the squares at 400 degrees for 7 to 8 minutes, until they are well browned, crisp, and glazed on top. Using a thin spatula, remove the squares from the cookie sheet, and cool them on a rack.

4. At serving time, place a phyllo square on each of four plates. Using a spoon, scrape a shaving of ice cream (about 1 ounce) for each serving and mound the shavings on top of the phyllo squares on the plates. Stack another phyllo square on top of each ice cream mound, and add another shaving of ice cream. Top the desserts with the remaining phyllo squares, and sprinkle on the remaining 1½ teaspoons of confectioners' sugar as a decoration, if desired. Serve immediately.

YIELD: 4 SERVINGS

Nutritional analysis per serving:

Calories 227	Fat 7.8 gm.
Protein 5 gm.	Saturated fat 2.9 gm.
Carbohydrates 33 gm.	Cholesterol 10 mg.
Sodium 127 mg.	

MERINGUE CHOCOLATE MOUSSE

BOILED MERINGUE

- 3 egg whites
- ½ cup sugar
- 3 tablespoons water

CHOCOLATE MIXTURE

- ⅓ cup cocoa powder
- ½ cup strong espresso coffee
- 2 teaspoons granulated gelatin
- 1 teaspoon grated lemon rind

Cookies (optional)

In place of the standard chocolate mousse ingredients—chocolate, whipped cream, egg yolks, and butter—I combine cocoa powder, which doesn't contain any fat, espresso coffee, and a little gelatin with a boiled meringue for this creamy dessert. Often used on its own as a cake frosting, the meringue mixture is made by cooking sugar and water to a soft-ball stage and combining it with egg whites. Covered tightly with plastic wrap so that it doesn't pick up the tastes of other foods, the mousse will keep for a few days in the refrigerator.

FOR THE BOILED MERINGUE

1. Place the egg whites in a mixer bowl, then set the bowl in a mixer fitted with a whisk attachment.

2. Place the sugar and water in a small unlined copper or stainless steel saucepan, and mix just enough to combine them. Bring to a boil over medium to high heat without stirring, and cover the pan.

3. Immediately start beating the egg whites at medium to high speed. Continue cooking the sugar mixture, covered, over medium to high heat for 1 minute to melt any crystals of sugar that have collected around the sides of the saucepan. Then remove the pan lid, and cook the mixture over medium to high heat for 3 to 3½ minutes, or until it registers 240 degrees (soft-ball stage) on a candy thermometer and becomes a syrup.

4. At this point, the egg whites should be firm and glossy, but not grainy. While you continue to beat the whites, pour the syrup from the pan in a steady thin stream (thread) into the middle of the bowl (avoiding the whisk). Continue beating the whites for about 2 minutes longer at medium to high speed. The mixture should be glossy and elastic. Set it aside to cool to room temperature.

FOR THE CHOCOLATE MIXTURE

5. Combine the cocoa powder, espresso, and gelatin in a medium saucepan. Bring the mixture to a boil over medium to high heat, stirring constantly. Set aside until cooled to room temperature, about 5 minutes.

6. Add the cooled chocolate mixture to the meringue, and fold it in gently but thoroughly with a whisk. Pour the mousse into a serving bowl. (You should have about 2½ cups.) Cover the bowl with plastic wrap, and refrigerate it for at least 3 hours or overnight.

7. To serve the mousse, scoop it into individual bowls, and sprinkle each with a little grated lemon rind. If desired, serve with cookies.

YIELD: 4 SERVINGS

Nutritional analysis per serving:

Calories 131	Fat 1.0 gm.
Protein 5 gm.	Saturated fat 0.6 gm.
Carbohydrates 29 gm.	Cholesterol 0 mg.
Sodium 46 mg.	

CARAMEL CUPS WITH COFFEE FROZEN YOGURT

¼ teaspoon canola oil

⅓ cup sugar

2 tablespoons water

1 pint low-fat or nonfat coffee frozen yogurt

Crystallized Mint Leaves or Rose Petals (see page 161)

 Caramel cups, used here as receptacles for frozen yogurt, make this dessert something of a showstopper. When making the cups, you have to stop the cooking of the caramel immediately after it reaches a rich brown color. The best way to do this and help the caramel mixture thicken to the right consistency is to dip the base of the pan containing the hot caramel into a bowl of cold water for a few seconds.

Drizzled over inverted small glass bowls that have been lightly oiled, the caramel hardens in 5 minutes and can be lifted off. The cups will keep in dry weather for up to a week, but they become sticky within a few hours if exposed to humidity. (See photograph, page 159.)

1. Lightly oil the outside of four small ovenproof glass bowls (6-ounce capacity), and place them upside down 3 to 4 inches apart on a cookie sheet lined with parchment paper.

FOR THE CARAMEL
2. Place the sugar and water in a medium saucepan of unlined copper or stainless steel. Stir just enough to combine them, bring the mixture to a boil over medium heat, and continue boiling until it turns a deep caramel color. Immediately dip the base of the saucepan into a bowl of cold water, and hold it there for about 10 seconds to stop the cooking of the caramel.

3. Stir the caramel with a metal spoon; it should thicken. When it is the consistency of a thick syrup, spoon out about a teaspoon and drizzle it around the sides and across the bottom of one of the inverted bowls, letting it fall about 1 inch beyond the bowl all around. Repeat with the remaining caramel syrup, drizzling it over and around the remaining bowls in a net or grid pattern that is structurally sound.

4. Let the bowls sit for about 5 minutes, until the caramel hardens, then lift the caramel cups off. Place the cups upside down on a cutting board. Heat the blade of a sharp knife by holding it in the flame of a gas burner or laying it across the coils of an electric stove, and trim off any large threads of caramel extending beyond the edges of the cups. The cups can sit at room temperature for a few hours before serving. Sealed in a plastic container, they will keep for up to a week if the weather is not humid. In humid weather, they will keep for only a few hours before becoming sticky.

5. To serve, place a caramel cup on each of four dessert plates. Fill the cups with softened frozen yogurt, and decorate the plates with a few crystallized mint leaves or rose petals. (If you prefer, you can double the caramel recipe and make eight cups instead of four. Then invert a second cup over each dessert to create a cage effect.) Serve immediately.

YIELD: 4 SERVINGS

Nutritional analysis per serving:

Calories 179	Fat 1.3 gm.
Protein 3 gm.	Saturated fat 0 gm.
Carbohydrates 39 gm.	Cholesterol 4 mg.
Sodium 0 mg.	

WHITE PEACH AND WALNUT TART

TART DOUGH
⅔ cup all-purpose flour
2 tablespoons unsalted butter
1 tablespoon corn oil
⅛ teaspoon salt
½ teaspoon sugar
1 tablespoon cold water

WALNUT MIXTURE
¼ cup walnut pieces
1 tablespoon all-purpose flour
1 tablespoon sugar
Dough trimmings

3 ripe white peaches (about
    1 pound), cut into quarters
¼ cup apricot preserves

 White peaches, one of my favorite fruits, are baked here in a tart shell created from a dough containing a minimum of flour and butter. To absorb some of the peach juices and lend added flavor to the tart, the shell and the peaches are sprinkled before baking with a mixture of walnuts, flour, and sugar, ground together with the dough trimmings into a powder. The baked dessert is glazed, while still warm, with a coating of jam and served at room temperature.

1. Preheat the oven to 400 degrees.

FOR THE TART DOUGH
2. Place all the dough ingredients except the water in the bowl of a food processor. Process for about 15 seconds, just until the mixture looks sandy. Add the water, and process for another 5 seconds, just until the mixture begins to gather together. Transfer the dough to a piece of plastic wrap and, using the wrap, gather the dough into a ball. Roll the dough between two sheets of plastic wrap until it is about 10 inches in diameter (it will be very thin). Place an 8-inch metal flan ring or removable-bottom quiche or tart pan on a cookie sheet, and fit the dough inside the ring, pressing it into place. Trim the top edge to remove any excess dough, and reserve the trimmings.

FOR THE WALNUT MIXTURE
3. Place all the walnut mixture ingredients, including the dough trimmings, in the bowl of a food processor. Process until well combined, and set aside.

4. Spread half of the walnut mixture on the bottom of the tart shell. Arrange the peach quarters in one layer, skin side down, around the circumference of the shell. (You should have two peach quarters remaining.) Cut each of the remaining peach quarters in half and arrange them skin side down, in the middle of the tart shell. Sprinkle the rest of the walnut mixture evenly on top.

5. Bake the tart at 400 degrees for 1 hour. Cool to lukewarm on a cooling rack, and then, using a spoon, spread the apricot preserves carefully over the top. Remove the ring from around the tart (the dough will shrink enough in cooking to allow easy removal).

6. Using two large hamburger spatulas, transfer the tart to a serving platter. Cut it into six wedges, and serve at room temperature. Refrigerate any leftovers, and enjoy them the next day.

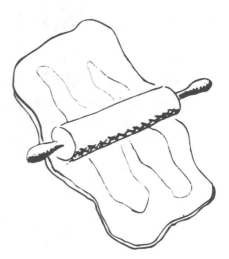

YIELD: 4 SERVINGS

Nutritional analysis per serving:

Calories 312	Fat 14.1 gm.
Protein 4 gm.	Saturated fat 4.4 gm.
Carbohydrates 45 gm.	Cholesterol 16 mg.
Sodium 79 mg.	

Tartelettes aux Fruits Panachés

⅔ cup all-purpose flour, plus a little flour for use in rolling out the dough

3 tablespoons cold unsalted butter, cut into 3 equal pieces

1 tablespoon canola oil

½ teaspoon sugar

⅛ teaspoon salt

1 tablespoon ice water, if needed

4 small ripe apricots (8 to 10 ounces)

4 small ripe dark plums (8 to 10 ounces)

2 tablespoons sugar

A minimum of flour and butter is used in the dough for these small, flavorful fruits panachés, or mixed fruit, tarts. A thin dough cut into disks is baked with a topping of lightly sugared apricot and plum wedges until the pastry is crisp and the fruit soft. (See photograph, page 157.)

1. Preheat the oven to 400 degrees.

2. Place the flour, butter, oil, ½ teaspoon sugar, and salt in the bowl of a food processor, and process for about 10 seconds. Feel the dough; if it is soft enough to gather together into a ball, remove it from the bowl, and form a ball. If it is still dry to the touch, add the ice water, and process for another 5 or 6 seconds before removing the dough from the bowl and forming a ball. Refrigerate the dough or roll it out immediately.

3. Lightly flour a flat work surface, and roll the ball of dough into a very thin layer (no more than ⅛ inch thick). Using a round cutter with a 5-inch diameter, cut four disks, gathering up and rerolling the trimmings as required. Carefully transfer the disks to a large cookie sheet or jelly roll pan, leaving a few inches of space between them.

4. Cut the apricots and plums into thin wedges, and arrange them alternating in a wedge spiral on top of each dough disk. Sprinkle the fruit with the 2 tablespoons of sugar, and bake the *tartelettes* at 400 degrees for 30 to 35 minutes, until the fruit is soft and the dough cooked through and nicely browned. Some of the juice from the fruit will have leaked out onto the cookie sheet. Before it hardens and makes the disks stick to the sheet, lift the tarts with a broad spatula, and transfer them to a cooling rack or platter.

5. At serving time, place a *tartelette* on each of four dessert plates, and serve lukewarm or at room temperature.

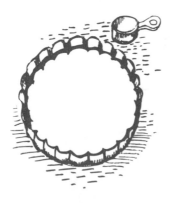

YIELD: 4 SERVINGS

Nutritional analysis per serving:

Calories 277	Fat 12.8 gm.
Protein 4 gm.	Saturated fat 5.7 gm.
Carbohydrates 39 gm.	Cholesterol 23 mg.
Sodium 71 mg.	

BREADS AND BASICS

INTRODUCTORY COMMENTS ON BREADS

In the recipes that follow, I present five different breads made with variations on the basic dough used traditionally for standard French breads. Included are a Large Country Bread (see page 182), which contains wheat bran; a Farmer Bread (see page 183), made with both wheat bran and rye flour; a Farmer Bread with Mixed Leavening (see page 184), made with leftover dough instead of yeast; a *Gros Pain* (see page 186), which means "big bread" in French and is a version of the standard large loaves made there with plain white flour; and Long-Proofed Baguettes (see page 187), which contain wheat bran, bulgur wheat, and a limited amount of yeast, so they are proofed (allowed to rise) longer.

By definition, the longer bread is proofed, the longer it will keep. When I was a child growing up in France during the Second World War, older farmers made bread without any leavening agents at all. There are some wild yeast cells in flour, although the quantities are relatively minute: while one gram ($\frac{1}{28}$ ounce) of fresh yeast is composed of several billion live yeast cells, one pound of flour contains only about ten thousand wild yeast cells. Granted, this represents an enormous difference, but if you keep "feeding" a flour-and-water "starter" with more flour, as was done by farmers years ago, the wild yeast cells develop, multiply, and, eventually, create a dough.

Commercial yeast has been available in France since the seventeenth century and has been used by professional bakers since then. Yet some country bakers still make bread with a *levain,* using only wild yeast. When creating the recipes for this book, I found I liked the results I got when I used a minimum of packaged yeast and let the dough proof a long time. The resulting loaves have a thick, crusty exterior and will stay fresh—at least the larger loaves—for up to a week if stored in plastic bags.

For conventional French loaves, the dough is always composed of flour, water, yeast, and a little salt. In addition to these basic ingredients, to some of my doughs I have added light, healthful wheat bran, which is the covering of the wheat grain. Bulgur wheat—cooked wheat berries—also is used in one of the recipes, and rye flour appears in the two farmer breads, which are characteristically darker in France. I use granulated yeast, available in envelopes at supermarkets.

The quality of the finished loaves is determined by several factors, among them the amount of time the dough is proofed and the temperature at which it is proofed. After mixing, bread dough should not exceed 70 to 75 degrees and should be proofed at a room temperature of 68 to 70 degrees. The amount of gluten (protein) in the flour also has a bearing on the outcome. In the recipes that follow, I use unbleached all-purpose flour, which contains between 9 and 12 percent gluten.

The ingredients can be combined and "kneaded" in a heavy-duty mixer with a dough hook, if you have one. Otherwise, prepare the dough in a food processor, which works especially well if yours, like mine, has variable speeds, but will do an adequate job even if it doesn't. The food processor I use is a large one; if yours is small, divide the ingredients in half, and mix the bread in two batches.

Traditionally, *boulangeries* (French bakery shops) make a "sponge" with yeast, a little flour, and some water, proof it for a few hours, and then add flour to create the final dough for the bread. This "sponge" method enables the baker to produce a great quantity of bread in relatively small space.

Here, I use the direct method—mixing everything together at once—because the goal is to create a single batch of bread. For one of the loaves, the Farmer Bread with Mixed Leavening (see page 184), I use a piece of dough reserved from a batch of bread made previously. The reserved dough, which will keep for 4 to 5 days in the refrigerator, serves as a leavening agent in this recipe, eliminating the need for any yeast if the dough is proofed, as it is here, for a long time—as long as 24 hours.

The remaining recipes, containing granulated yeast, are proofed for at least 4 hours, although they can proof longer, as

the Farmer Bread does (see page 183). It works very well to let the dough proof slowly at room temperature overnight, then shape it in the morning, and let it rise an additional 1½ hours before baking it. It takes 1½ hours to bake the large single loaves at a high temperature. For best results, let the large loaves rest for at least 3 hours before slicing them.

Although the bread dough can be proofed in any large, deep container, I use large plastic buckets with lids that I obtained from my fishmonger. These are large enough so I can shape a loaf in the bucket, place the loaf on a tray for final proofing, and invert the bucket over it to serve as a kind of "hothouse" in which the dough proofs.

I like to line the cookie sheets or baking trays with parchment paper and then sprinkle them with a little semolina, farina, oatmeal, or cornmeal to add a light coating to the bottom of the bread. The advantages of the paper are that it keeps the pans clean and provides a surface from which the baked bread slides off easily. In addition, if you bake bread on a bread or pizza stone (which I often do since I have a stone on a rack in my oven at home), you can slide the paper with the proofed loaf directly onto the stone for baking.

Professional ovens used for bread baking have the capacity to inject steam as the bread bakes. This helps proof the bread, enabling it to "push up" in a sense at the beginning and cook quickly. I attempt to duplicate these conditions and create the same effect by throwing a little water on the floor of my oven at the beginning of the cooking process.

At first I cook the bread at a very high temperature; then I reduce the temperature in most instances and continue cooking the loaves for a long time. When properly cooked, bread reaches an internal temperature of approximately 210 degrees.

It's fun to make homemade bread. Delicious as is for the first few days after baking, it makes great toast when it begins to dry out a little.

LARGE COUNTRY BREAD

4½ cups unbleached all-purpose
    flour (1½ pounds), plus
    2 tablespoons for sprinkling
    on the work surface and the
    loaves
 ½ cup wheat bran (½ ounce)
1½ teaspoons granulated yeast
 2 teaspoons salt
 2 cups cool bottled water or
    spring water (approximately
    70 degrees)
 1 tablespoon yellow cornmeal
 1 tablespoon tap water

See photograph, page 123.

**YIELD: 1 LOAF
(ABOUT 2 POUNDS BAKED)**

Nutritional analysis per loaf:
Calories 2,616   Fat 7.8 gm.
Protein 77 gm.   Saturated fat 1.2 gm.
Carbohydrates 550 gm. Cholesterol 0 mg.
Sodium 4,419 mg.

1. Place the 4½ cups flour, the wheat bran, yeast, salt, and the bottled water in a mixer or food processor bowl fitted with a blade. Mix at low speed for about 45 seconds; the dough should be satiny and elastic and no warmer than about 75 degrees. (It will weigh about 2 pounds 10 ounces.)

2. Place the dough in a plastic bucket, cover it, and set it aside to proof at room temperature (68 to 70 degrees) for 4 hours.

3. After rising for 4 hours, the dough should have tripled in volume. Break it down by bringing its outer edges into the center of the bowl and pressing down on the dough to release the air inside. Cover the dough again, and allow it to proof for another 2 hours. Then break it down again the same way.

4. Sprinkle 1 tablespoon of the remaining flour on your work surface. Place the dough on the floured surface, and form it into a large ball, stretching and tucking the sides underneath, to make the top smooth and taut. Press on the top of the ball lightly with the palm of one hand to push the air out.

5. Line a large cookie sheet with parchment paper, sprinkle it with the cornmeal, and place the ball of dough seam side down on the sheet. Cover it with the inverted bucket, and let it proof at room temperature for 1¼ to 1½ hours.

6. After 1 to 1¼ hours, preheat the oven to 425 degrees.

7. Sprinkle the top of the proofed loaf with the remaining tablespoon of flour, and cut several slits across the top of the loaf with a serrated knife. Place the loaf in the oven and throw the 1 tablespoon of tap water on the floor of the oven (to create steam) immediately before closing the door. Bake for 15 minutes, then reduce the oven heat to 400 degrees, and cook the loaf for 1 hour longer, until it is nicely browned and makes a hollow sound when you tap it.

8. Cool the loaf on a rack at room temperature for about 3 hours before cutting it into slices for serving. Wrapped in plastic wrap, the bread will keep for 4 to 5 days. It can also be frozen.

FARMER BREAD

4 cups unbleached all-purpose
   flour (1 pound, 5 ounces), plus
   1 teaspoon for sprinkling on
   the loaves
½ cup rye flour (about 3 ounces)
½ cup wheat bran (½ ounce)
2½ teaspoons salt
1 teaspoon granulated yeast
2⅓ cups cool tap water or bottled
   water (approximately 70
   degrees), plus 1 tablespoon to
   throw on the oven floor
2 tablespoons cornmeal

See photograph, page 123.

**YIELD: 1 LARGE LOAF
(ABOUT 2 POUNDS BAKED)**

Nutritional analysis per loaf:
Calories 2,615   Fat 9.1 gm.
Protein 77 gm.   Saturated fat 1.4 gm.
Carbohydrates 556 gm.   Cholesterol 0 mg.
Sodium 5,513 mg.

1. Place the 4 cups unbleached flour, the rye flour, bran, salt, yeast, and 2⅓ cups water in a mixer bowl, and mix at low speed for 3 to 4 minutes to create a smooth dough. Alternatively, place the ingredients in the bowl of a food processor, and process for about 45 seconds. (The dough will weigh about 2 pounds 10 ounces.)

2. Transfer the dough to a deep glass or ceramic bowl or a plastic bucket, cover tightly with a lid or plastic wrap, and let rise at room temperature (about 65 degrees) overnight (12 to 14 hours).

3. Bring the sides of the risen dough into the center of the bowl, folding it in on itself, and press down on the dough to release the air inside. Form the dough into a ball. Line a cookie sheet with parchment paper, sprinkle it with the cornmeal, and place the ball of dough seam side down in the center. Invert the bowl or bucket over the dough. (The bowl or bucket should be deep and wide enough so that the dough does not touch and stick to it as it rises.) Let the dough rise at room temperature for 1½ hours.

4. Near the end of the proofing period, preheat the oven to 425 degrees.

5. Sprinkle the risen loaf with the teaspoon of flour and, using a serrated knife, cut several decorative slits across the top of the loaf. Place the loaf in the oven, and throw the 1 tablespoon of water on the floor of the oven (to create steam) immediately before closing the door. Bake the loaf for 15 minutes, then reduce the heat to 400 degrees, and cook the loaf for 1 hour longer.

6. Remove the bread from the cookie sheet, place it on a wire rack, and cool it at room temperature for about 3 hours before cutting it into slices for serving. Wrapped in plastic wrap, the bread will keep for 4 to 5 days. It can also be frozen.

FARMER BREAD WITH MIXED LEAVENING

10 ounces leftover dough from a previous batch of bread (see Introductory Comments on Breads, page 179)

4½ cups unbleached all-purpose flour (1½ pounds), plus 1 teaspoon for sprinkling on the loaf

1 cup wheat bran (1 ounce)

½ cup rye flour (about 3 ounces)

2½ teaspoons salt

2 cups cool water (approximately 70 degrees), plus 2 tablespoons to throw on the oven floor

2 tablespoons oatmeal flakes or cornmeal

See photograph, page 123.

1. Mix the leftover dough, 4½ cups flour, wheat bran, rye flour, salt, and 2 cups cool water at low speed in a mixer fitted with a bread hook for 4 to 5 minutes. Alternatively, place the ingredients in the bowl of a large food processor, and process them at low to medium speed (if your processor has variable speeds) for 45 seconds. (The dough will weigh about 3 pounds 5 ounces.)

2. Transfer the dough to a plastic bucket, cover it with the lid, and proof it at room temperature (65 to 70 degrees) for at least 12 hours and as long as 24 hours (remember, there is no yeast in the recipe).

3. Break down the risen dough by bringing its outer edges into the center of the bowl and pressing down on the dough to release the air inside. Form the dough into a large round or oval loaf, tucking the sides underneath and seaming them so the loaf is smooth and taut on top.

4. Sprinkle the oatmeal evenly in the center of a cookie sheet, and place the bread loaf seam side down in the middle of the sheet. Invert the plastic bucket over the loaf, and let it rise at room temperature for 2 hours.

5. After about 1¾ hours, preheat the oven to 425 degrees.

6. Sprinkle the proofed loaf with the remaining teaspoon of flour, and cut several decorative slits across the top of the loaf with a serrated knife or razor.

7. Place the loaf in the oven, and throw 1 tablespoon of water on the floor of the oven (to create steam) immediately before closing the door. Bake the bread for 5 minutes, then throw another tablespoon of water on the floor of the oven, and bake for 15 minutes longer. Reduce the oven temperature to 400 degrees, and continue baking the loaf for 1 hour, until it is brown and sounds hollow when tapped.

8. Cool the bread on a rack for at least 3 hours before cutting it into slices and serving. The loaf will keep for at least 5 days if wrapped tightly in a cloth bag (an old pillow case, perhaps) or longer if enclosed in a plastic bag. It can also be frozen.

**YIELD: 1 LARGE LOAF
(ABOUT 2½ POUNDS BAKED)**

Nutritional analysis per loaf:

Calories 3,517	Fat 11.9 gm.
Protein 103 gm.	Saturated fat 1.8 gm.
Carbohydrates 745 gm.	Cholesterol 0 mg.
Sodium 6,573 mg.	

GROS PAIN

4½ cups unbleached all-purpose flour (1½ pounds), plus 3 tablespoons for kneading purposes and for sprinkling on the loaves

2½ teaspoons salt

1 envelope granulated yeast (about 2 teaspoons)

2 cups cool water (approximately 70 degrees), plus 2 tablespoons to throw on the oven floor

1 tablespoon cornmeal or farina

See photograph, page 123.

See photograph, page 123.

YIELD: 1 LARGE LOAF (ABOUT 2 POUNDS BAKED)

Nutritional analysis per loaf:

Calories 2,616	Fat 7.2 gm.
Protein 76 gm.	Saturated fat 1.1 gm.
Carbohydrates 547 gm.	Cholesterol 0 mg.
Sodium 5,513 mg.	

1. Place the 4½ cups flour, salt, yeast, and 2 cups water in the bowl of a large food processor. Process the mixture for about 45 seconds on low speed if your processor has variable speeds, or about 30 seconds if your processor has only one speed. (The temperature of the dough should not exceed 75 degrees.) (The dough will weigh about 2½ pounds.)

2. Transfer the dough to a large, deep ceramic or stainless steel bowl or a plastic bucket (preferable), cover tightly with a lid or plastic wrap, and set aside to rise at room temperature (65 to 70 degrees) for 5 hours.

3. Break down the dough by bringing its outer edges into the center of the bowl and pressing down to release the air inside. Then lift the dough from the bucket with one hand, and sprinkle 2 tablespoons of the flour into the bucket with the other. Return the ball of dough to the bucket, and knead it until the flour is incorporated and the dough has elasticity, about 1 minute. Form the dough into a ball, stretching and seaming it underneath so it is nicely rounded and taut on top.

4. Line a large cookie sheet with parchment paper, and sprinkle the cornmeal on top. Place the dough seam side down on the sheet, and cover it with the overturned bowl or bucket. Set the loaf aside to rise at room temperature for 2 hours.

5. After about 1¾ hours, preheat the oven to 425 degrees.

6. Sprinkle the top of the proofed loaf with the remaining tablespoon of flour, and cut several slits across the top of the loaf with a serrated knife. Place the loaf in the oven, and throw 1 tablespoon of water on the floor of the oven (to create steam) immediately before closing the door. After 5 minutes, throw another tablespoon of water on the oven floor. Bake the loaf for 15 minutes more at 425 degrees, then reduce the oven temperature to 400 degrees, and bake for 1 hour longer.

7. Cool the bread on a rack for at least 3 hours, then slice and serve it.

LONG-PROOFED BAGUETTES

4½ cups unbleached all-purpose flour (1½ pounds), plus 2½ tablespoons for sprinkling on the work surface and the loaves

½ cup wheat bran (½ ounce)

½ cup bulgur wheat (2½ ounces)

2 teaspoons granulated yeast

2½ teaspoons salt

2¼ cups cool water (approximately 70 degrees), plus 1 tablespoon to throw on the oven floor

2 tablespoons cornmeal

See photograph, page 123.

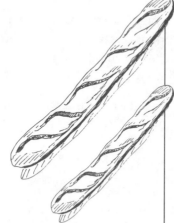

YIELD: 4 BAGUETTES (ABOUT 8 OUNCES EACH BAKED)

Nutritional analysis per baguette:

Calories 727	Fat 2.2 gm.
Protein 22 gm.	Saturated fat 0.3 gm.
Carbohydrates 153 gm.	Cholesterol 0 mg.
Sodium 1,382 mg.	

1. Place the 4½ cups of flour, wheat bran, bulgur wheat, yeast, salt, and 2¼ cups water in a mixer bowl, and mix with a bread hook at low speed for 3 to 5 minutes. Alternatively, place the ingredients in the bowl of a large food processor, and process at medium speed (if your processor has variable speeds) for 45 seconds. (The dough will weigh about 2 pounds 12 ounces.)

2. Transfer the dough to a large, deep ceramic or stainless steel bowl or a plastic bucket, cover, and let rise at room temperature (65 to 70 degrees) for at least 4½ hours.

3. Break down the dough by bringing its outer edges into the center of the bowl and pressing down to release the air inside. Form the dough into a ball. Sprinkle your work surface with 2 tablespoons of the remaining flour, place the ball of dough on top, and press down to form it into a rough rectangular shape. Cut the rectangle lengthwise into 4 equal strips, and roll each strip into an 18-inch length.

4. Sprinkle four metal baguette molds with the cornmeal, dividing it as evenly as possible among the molds, and place a dough strip in each mold. Cover the molds with plastic wrap, and let the bread rise for 1 hour at room temperature.

5. After about 50 minutes, preheat the oven to 425 degrees.

6. Sprinkle the tops of the risen loaves with the remaining ½ tablespoon of flour, and cut four diagonal slits on the top surface of each loaf with a serrated knife or razor blade.

7. Arrange the molds on a cookie sheet or tray, place them in the oven, and throw 1 tablespoon of water on the floor of the oven (to create steam) immediately before closing the door. Bake the baguettes for 35 minutes.

8. Remove the baguettes from the molds, and cool them on a rack for at least 45 minutes before slicing and serving. Wrapped in plastic wrap, the loaves will keep for about 48 hours.

BASIC CHICKEN STOCK

3 pounds chicken bones (necks, backs, and gizzards, skinless or with as little skin as possible)

6 quarts lukewarm tap water

1 tablespoon *herbes de Provence* (see page 190)

1 large onion (about 8 ounces), peeled and quartered

12 whole cloves

4 bay leaves

1 tablespoon dark soy sauce

Stock is used throughout this book in soups, sauces, stews, and other recipes. It takes very little work to make your own stock; mostly it is a matter of staying home for the several hours it takes to cook. Chicken backs and necks are now available packaged at most supermarkets. If you don't see them, ask a butcher there to package some for you, or buy turkey backs, necks, and gizzards instead. From a health standpoint, it is well worth making your own stock, since it will be practically fat-free and salt-free. A flavorful money saver, it can be frozen in small quantities and used as needed.

1. Place the bones and water in a large stockpot, and bring to a boil over high heat. Reduce the heat, and boil gently for 30 minutes. Most of the fat and impurities will rise to the surface during this time; skim off as much of them as you can, and discard them.

2. Add the remainder of the ingredients, return the liquid to a boil, and boil gently for 2½ hours. Strain the stock through a fine-mesh strainer or a colander lined with a dampened kitchen towel or paper towels.

3. Allow the stock to cool. Then remove the surface fat, and freeze the stock in plastic containers with tight lids.

YIELD: 3 QUARTS (12 CUPS)

Nutritional analysis per cup:

Calories 36	Fat 1.5 gm.
Protein 2 gm.	Saturated fat 0.4 gm.
Carbohydrates 3 gm.	Cholesterol 0 mg.
Sodium 140 mg.	

TARRAGON OIL

2 cups water, for blanching
1 cup (lightly packed) fresh
   tarragon leaves
½ teaspoon salt
1 cup corn, canola, or
   peanut oil

Herb-flavored oils have added a new dimension to salads and stews, and they are delicious brushed on grilled meat, fish, or poultry (see the alternative for finishing Grilled Chicken with Tarragon Butter on page 80). It is important that the tarragon leaves used in this preparation retain their bright green color. To achieve this, blanch them first, which wilts them and locks in their color. Chop the tarragon by hand for a few seconds to break it down a little, then puree it in a mini-chop or blender, which works much better than a food processor for this purpose. The leaf puree will retain its bright green color and fresh flavor in the oil.

1. Bring the water to a boil in a saucepan. Add the tarragon leaves, stir, and cook for about 30 seconds, or just until the water returns to a boil again.

2. Drain the leaves in a strainer, and rinse them under cool tap water. Chop them coarsely with a sharp knife, and then place them in the bowl of a mini-chop or blender with the salt and ½ cup of the oil. Process until thoroughly blended, and transfer to a mixing bowl. Stir in the remaining oil, and refrigerate until ready to use.

YIELD: 1 CUP

Nutritional analysis per tablespoon:

Calories 124	Fat 13.7 gm.
Protein 0.3 gm.	Saturated fat 1.7 gm.
Carbohydrates 0.6 gm.	Cholesterol 0 mg.
Sodium 69 mg.	

HERBES DE PROVENCE

REQUIRED HERBS
Thyme
Savory
Marjoram
Oregano

OPTIONAL HERBS
Sage
Rosemary
Lavender flowers
Fennel seeds

 Herbes de Provence is a blend of dried herbs that is used frequently in the cooking of southern France. This blend always contains thyme, savory, marjoram, and oregano in equal proportions, but lesser amounts of other herbs can also be included. Herbes de Provence is readily available commercially in Provence and elsewhere in the Mediterranean basin, and it can be purchased in many specialty food stores here. It is similar to Italian seasoning, which can be found in most American supermarkets and is a good substitute.

In response to numerous requests from Today's Gourmet viewers who have been unable to find herbes de Provence in their area, I have devised a recipe for a homemade version of this aromatic herb blend made with fresh herbs that you dry yourself. If fresh herbs aren't available at all or only some of those listed are available, you can make your herbes de Provence mixture by combining commercially produced dried herbs in the proportions indicated below.

FOR THE REQUIRED HERBS

1. Dry the leaves of fresh thyme, savory, marjoram, and oregano by arranging them (one herb variety at a time) in a single layer on one or more cookie sheets and placing them in a low oven (180 degrees) until dry (12 to 20 minutes, depending on the herbs), or air dry them outdoors in the summer shade.

2. Mix together equal amounts of the dried herbs.

FOR THE OPTIONAL HERBS

3. Dry the sage and rosemary leaves and the lavender flowers as indicated above. Mix together equal proportions of these herbs with a like amount of fennel seeds.

4. Following a 2-to-1 formula, mix a whole portion of the required herbs mixture with a half portion of the optional herbs mixture. Enclose in plastic bags, sealing them tightly to preserve the freshness of the herbs. Use in recipes as needed.

Nutritional analysis per teaspoon:

Calories 3	Fat 0.1 gm.
Protein 0.1 gm.	Saturated fat 0 gm.
Carbohydrates 0.8 gm.	Cholesterol 0 mg.
Sodium 0 mg.	

HEALTH NOTES

To me, modern cuisine is really commonsense cuisine. Today's menus should consist of foods that are tasty and beautiful, as well as a variety of foods that help to maintain healthy weight. Meals should be low in fat, saturated fat, and cholesterol, contain plenty of vegetables, fruits, and grain products, and include sugars, salt, and alcohol in moderation.

TECHNIQUES AND EQUIPMENT

I have found that using certain techniques and equipment in the kitchen can enhance the nutritional value of foods. For instance, fats are the most calorie-laden food that we eat. With few exceptions, any techniques and equipment that reduce our fat intake will improve our diet.

One excellent way to cut down on fats in cooking is to use nonstick pans. The amount of fat used to sauté in a nonstick pan is less than half of what might be used in an untreated pan. I like to use nonstick pans with a permanent finish when I sauté and fry.

Grilling is another great way to enhance the flavor of foods without adding fat or sodium. There is great diversity in the types of grills available today. When I grill, I like to use natural wood chips such as apple wood, olive wood, or cherry wood for their delicious smoky flavor and ability to produce high heat. I often use wood charcoal because it is precooked so it turns to hot coal quickly. Charcoal briquettes are petroleum based and should be reduced to a gray ash color before you cook over them. This reduces the tar flavor that food can pick up from them.

VITAMINS AND MINERALS

For years we have been concerned about the amounts of vitamins and minerals in our diet. Modern cooking has given us some new insight into this old subject.

We now know that the old way of cooking vegetables, which was to blanch them in large pots of boiling water and then refresh them in cold water before seasoning, resulted in the loss of essential vitamins and minerals. I recommend cooking vegetables in a small amount of boiling water just until the water disappears, thus retaining maximum amounts of vitamins and minerals.

Iron intake is a particular concern for many people, especially women. Many of my recipes, such as Gratin of Breaded Oysters (page 51), Grilled Lamb Chops Riviera (page 96), and Chili con Carne with Red Beans (page 105) are high in iron.

PROTEIN

Red meat, long maligned as a high-fat protein source, has moved into the nineties as a much lighter main course item. Now that steers and pigs are being raised to produce leaner meat, we can get our iron and protein from these red meat sources without worrying about fat intake. When we trim the meat properly before cooking and serve smaller portions, red meat is part of a healthy gourmet diet. For example, my recipes for Grilled Pork *Paillards* with Rosemary (page 91) and Venison Steaks in Sweet-Sour Sauce (page 110) are high in protein and low in calories and fat.

FIBER

Today, experts recommend a diet high in fiber to help reduce cholesterol. For you and me, that means approximately 25 to 30 mg. of fiber per day. Luckily, water-soluble dietary fiber is contained in some delicious packages. Fiber is a part of plant foods. It is found in abundance in whole-grain breads and cereals, fresh and dried fruits, and vegetables. My menus all include these foods. Some recipes especially high in fiber are Barley-Stuffed Cabbage Rolls (page 94), Gratin of Ziti and Vegetables (page 36), and Lentil and Potato Salad (page 61).

COMPLEX CARBOHYDRATES

Complex carbohydrates, which give us long-lasting energy by slowly converting to sugars during digestion, do not necessarily need to be combined with high-fat foods to be delicious. Complex carbohydrates are found in many of the foods that also happen to be rich in fiber, vitamins, and minerals, such as whole grain breads, cereals, pasta, rice, beans, and potatoes.

WHOLE GRAINS

Adding whole grains to your diet is a great way to add protein, fiber, and complex carbohydrates. I often use traditional grains such as hominy in nontraditional ways. My Squid and *Posole* Hodgepodge (page 54) is a good example. Also I recommend using grains that are now gaining in popularity, such as polenta, featured with mushrooms on page 22.

CALORIES

Reducing calories does not necessarily mean eating tiny portions of trendy food. There are many hearty, filling dishes that are very low in calories. Some of these dishes in *Happy Cooking!* are: Slow-Cooked Roast of Lamb (page 98), *Garbure* Soup Farmer-Style (page 92), and Chicken *Ballottine* Stuffed with Red Rice (page 88).

I have suggested several dessert recipes that are quite low in calories, too. While a typical portion of dessert often contains as many as 500 calories per serving, the following desserts are much lighter and contain under 130 calories: Meringue Chocolate Mousse (page 170), Grapefruit in Nectar (page 148), and Raspberry Velvet (page 156).

On special occasions, we tend to consume a few more calories than we would during the rest of the year. I have suggested a menu for special guests that is delicious but contains approximately half the calories of a typical feast. It features Red Onion and Orange Salad (page 38), Osso Buco (page 106), Brown Saffron Rice (page 132), and Raspberry Trifle with Nectarine Sauce (page 152).

CHOLESTEROL

The American Heart Association recommends that we consume no more than 300 mg. of cholesterol per day. In most instances, I use oils instead of butter to cut down on cholesterol. In addition, my recipes minimize the number of egg yolks per serving, since yolks are high in cholesterol.

FATS AND LOW-FAT ALTERNATIVES

Experts believe that a healthy diet is one in which no more than 30 percent of the daily calories consumed are derived from the intake of fat. To achieve this percentage, I sometimes substitute low-fat alternatives in my recipes. For example, I may use nonfat or low-fat yogurt instead of sour cream.

Some fats have proved beneficial to health. Salmon, although it is a fatty fish, contains what are now described by experts as "heart-healthy fats," or omega-3s. These omega-3s help keep blood from getting "sticky" and forming clots that lead to heart attacks. Eating fatty fishes has also been correlated with lower levels of certain fats called triglycerides in the blood. Because of these benefits, health experts are urging us to eat more fish, up to 15 pounds per year. Fish is featured prominently in many of the menus in *Happy Cooking!*

OILS

Today's supermarket offers a vast selection of oils. It is important to understand the nature of oils to know which one to choose. For instance, some oils are lower in saturated fat than others, some are more strongly flavored, and some may burn at a relatively low temperature, giving off bad odors and flavor.

At room temperature, all oils are liquid fat. Some oils, such as palm and coconut oil, are very high in saturated fat and therefore can boost the level of blood cholesterol. In much of my cooking, I use the oil that is lowest in saturated fat—canola oil.

Virgin olive oil is usually dark, with a rich olive flavor. The color and flavor are the result of olive solids present in the oil. Virgin olive oil is so named because it has been removed from the olives by mechanical pressing, from the sheer weight of the olives. No heat or chemical processes are used to extract this oil. The olive solids, which impart flavor and color, burn at fairly low temperatures, so virgin olive oil is best used for salads and marinades.

The best oils to use in sautéing are flavorless safflower and canola oils, or, for mild flavor, peanut oil. They are ideal for sautéing because they can withstand high temperatures without burning.

SUGARS

It is important to use moderation when consuming refined sugar. Refined sugar can lead to tooth decay and, when combined with fat, can be tremendously caloric. But who can resist sweet treats on special occasions? For this reason, I have included recipes for White Peach and Walnut Tart (page 174), Ice-Cream Phyllo Napoleons (page 169), and Farina Bavarian Cream Cake with Apricot Sauce (page 166). A small bit of a rich dessert can help you to feel satisfied without over-doing it.

SALT

I have some special tips for cutting down on salt. Because I like highly seasoned foods, I use a variety of seasonings as salt substitutes. Plenty of fresh herbs and strong-flavored spices are excellent substitutes.

The key to reducing the amount of salt used in cooking is to bring out the natural flavor in the food itself. For example, if you crystallize the juices on the outside of meat by browning it well first, as I do in my Slow-Cooked Roast of Lamb recipe (page 98), you can bring up the flavor without adding an excess of salt. Another way to enhance flavor, featured in my Osso Buco (page 106), is to use citrus fruit, such as lemon or orange, or the numerous fresh herbs and spices available today. And don't forget about flavor-enhancing cooking techniques such as grilling, steaming, and broiling.

VEGETABLES

Vegetables are the most important kind of food to emphasize in our diets. They are naturally low in calories and high in fiber, vitamins, and minerals. Whenever possible, I buy organic fruits and vegetables for their fantastic flavor and guaranteed wholesomeness. My friend Alice Waters, of Chez Panisse restaurant, says that by purchasing organic fruits and vegetables we support the people who work to preserve and enhance our farmlands.

When I was young, my mother was an organic gardener, and she didn't even know it! But this was in a time when growing food without chemicals was a way of life, not a specialty. Today, both consumers and growers are returning to that natural approach to food.

ABOUT JACQUES PÉPIN

Jacques Pépin, master chef, author, and teacher to a generation of famous chefs as well as millions of enthusiastic home cooks, was born in Bourg-en-Bresse, near Lyon. His first exposure to cooking was in his parents' restaurant, Le Pélican. At age thirteen, he began his formal apprenticeship at the Grand Hôtel de l'Europe in his hometown.

He soon graduated to the Meurice in Paris and then the Plaza-Athenée, where he trained under Lucien Diat. From 1956 to 1958, he was personal chef to three French heads of state, including Charles de Gaulle.

Moving to the United States in 1959, Pépin went from New York's Le Pavillon restaurant to the Howard Johnson Company, where he was director of research and new development for ten years. He also earned a master's degree in eighteenth-century French literature from Columbia University.

For the past twenty years, Pépin has devoted his time to writing, teaching, and consulting. A frequent guest on radio and TV, he crisscrosses the country to teach and give demonstrations at cooking schools, fund-raising events, and culinary festivals. He writes a monthly column, "The Purposeful Cook," for the *New York Times* and a quarterly column, "Jacques' Favorite," for *Food & Wine,* where he is a contributing editor.

Today's Gourmet with Jacques Pépin debuted on PBS in January 1991 and quickly became one of the top-rated cooking shows on television. The two-part home video version of the series was recently awarded the James Beard Award for Best Culinary Video. The third season of *Today's Gourmet,* with the recipes and menus in *Happy Cooking!* began airing nationally in October 1994.

Pépin's best-selling cookbooks include the companion volumes to the first two seasons of the PBS series, *Today's Gourmet* and *Good Life Cooking* (KQED), *The Art of Cooking* (Knopf), *The Short-Cut Cook* (Morrow), and *Cuisine Economique* (Morrow). *Jacques Pépin's Light and Healthy Cooking* (Rodale) will be published in early 1995.

Pépin is Dean of Studies at the French Culinary Institute in New York City and teaches a graduate "Culture and Cuisine" course at Boston University, where he helped formulate a concentration in gastronomy that is now part of the school's Master of Liberal Arts program.

He is a founder of the American Institute of Wine and Food, is on the board of trustees of the James Beard Foundation, and is a member of the International Association of Culinary Professionals.

Jacques and his wife, Gloria, live in Madison, Connecticut. Their daughter, Claudine, lives in Boston

PRODUCER'S ACKNOWLEDGMENTS

Well over forty people and countless vendors joined energies to create the third season of *Today's Gourmet with Jacques Pépin*. From a veteran engineer who has been with KQED since 1954 to an unpaid volunteer who showed up every day and became assistant stylist, the entire production was a labor of love, creativity, and skill. Jacques's charm and staggering expertise were a great inspiration, and the same accessibility and good humor he displays on screen kept his staff and crew on track during a whirlwind schedule of taping twenty-six shows in only nine days.

All of this would have been impossible without our generous funders, who pitched in on many levels this year more than ever. Who would have expected the CEO of Russell Range to be on the loading dock in his workshirt, showing Jacques the fine points of the barbeque unit or helping our stage manager tighten the gas lines? An extra pair of helping hands belonged to Cambria Vineyards' executive chef, who came to visit bearing a huge basket of wild mushrooms, organic produce, and decorative platters to use on the air, and stayed on to work in the back kitchen for two days. (We lent him an apron.) Braun was kind enough to send an extra set of appliances to use backstage, and we found the espresso maker particularly helpful.

The Ritz-Carlton housed Jacques for his month in San Francisco in a style to which we would all like to become accustomed, and extended its welcome to his family as well. Gloria and Claudine Pépin and Jean-Claude Szurdak were wonderful on-camera guests. Levi Strauss opened the doors of its warehouse and sample room, outfitting Jacques impeccably. Retail stores and manufacturers of china and linens graced us with a huge array of props. Food purveyors were extremely generous, as were antique dealers who furnished the set, cookware manufacturers who provided the *batterie de cuisine* without which we simply could not have prepared all that food, and wine producers and distributors who gave Jacques the opportunity to toast his audience at the end of each episode.

Such examples of generosity are the foundation of public television. As Jacques likes to say, we enjoyed making it for you; and after a hearty thank you, we can only say, "Happy Cooking!"

—PEGGY LEE SCOTT

Today's Gourmet with Jacques Pépin thanks the following companies for their generous support of the third season's programs.

WINES PROVIDED BY:

Blair Importers
Boisset Wines USA
Bordeaux Wine Bureau
Cambria Vineyards & Winery
Dreyfus-Ashby & Co.
Kendall-Jackson Winery
Kermit Lynch Wine Merchant
Kobrand Corporation
Le Monjea Distingué Wine
    Importers
Seagram Chateau & Estate
    Wines Company
Seagram Classic Wine Company
Shaw-Ross International
    Importers
Val d'Orbieu Wines

FOOD PROVIDED BY:

BIRITE Foodservice Distributors
California Crayfish, Inc.
Greenleaf Produce
Modesto Food Distributors
C. J. Olson Cherries
United Meat Company, Inc.

SPECIAL THANKS TO:

Ritz-Carlton, San Francisco
Levi Strauss & Co.
All-Clad Metalcrafters
Ames Gallery
Angray Flowers
Berkeley Farmers' Market
Bernardaud
Biordi Art Imports
Bourgeat USA
Braun Inc.
Champagne News and
    Information Bureau
Chef'sChoice® by EdgeCraft
Dacor Ovens
Domestications Catalog
General Electric Appliances
George V Collection
Hartford Court Winery
Harvey Antiques
La Parisienne Posters
Macy's California
Oscartielle Equipment,
    California
Peoples Woods
Pier 1 Imports
Pierre Deux
Russell Range, Inc.
Saint-Louis Cristal—
    Hermès Art de la Table
Sakura, Inc.
Signature China
Terra Firma Farms
Westside Farms
Williams-Sonoma

TODAY'S
GOURMET III

INDEX

Page numbers in *italic* designate the menu that includes the dish; those in **bold** designate the photograph of the dish.

Page numbers in *italic* designate the menu that includes the dish; those in **bold** designate the photograph of the dish.

Page numbers in *italic* designate the menu that includes the dish; those in **bold** designate the photograph of the dish.

Page numbers in *italic* designate the menu that includes the dish; those in **bold** designate the photograph of the dish.

Page numbers in *italic* designate the menu that includes the dish; those in **bold** designate the photograph of the dish.

Swiss chard, red, with ginger, *14,* 133
Swordfish, grilled, with spicy yogurt
    sauce, *8,* 49

T

Tarragon:
    butter, grilled chicken with, 80, **83**
    and lemon sauce, calves' liver
        with, 100
    oil, 189
    and tomato sauce, for monkfish
        roulade, 68–69, **104**
Tart, white peach and walnut, *11,*
    174–75
Tartelettes aux fruits panachés, 4,
    157, 176
Techniques and equipment, 192
Timbales of shrimp and spinach, *6,*
    28, 60
Tomato(es):
    and avocado salad, *9,* 39
    and cider sauce, for cabbage rolls,
        94–95
    and eggplant, gratin of, *7,* **101,**
        126
    in red onion and orange salad, 38
    and red pepper sauce, stuffed
        zucchini "boats" with, 78–79
    sauce, spaghetti squash in,
        32–33, **48**
    and zucchini fans, *13,* **26,** 29
Trifle, raspberry, with nectarine
    sauce, *16,* 152–53
Trout, smoked, with scrambled eggs
    on toast, *8,* **46,** 50
Turkey, poached, in vegetable
    consommé, *8,* 90, **121**

V

Veal:
    chops, with olive shavings, *14,* 99

Veal—*continued*
    shanks, in osso buco, 106–7
Vegetable(s):
    bouquet on fettucine, *4,* **45,**
        86–87
    brunoise, codfish flakes in, 43
    consommé, poached turkey in,
        90, **121**
    cooking of, 192–93
    in diet, 196
    mirepoix (diced vegetables),
        flageolets in, 118
    and ziti, gratin of, *10,* 36–37
Venison steaks in sweet-sour sauce,
    15, **84,** 110–11
Vitamins, 192–93

W

Walnut:
    sausage, *7,* 62
    and white peach tart, *11,* 174–75
White peach and walnut tart, *11,*
    174–75
Wine, red, sauce:
    for chicken *ballottine,* 89
    mushroom-stuffed wontons in,
        34–35
Wontons:
    for crab ravioli, 72–73
    mushroom-stuffed, in red wine
        sauce, *11,* 34–35
    shells for lemon bananas, 142–43

Y

Yam, for skillet sweet potatoes, 130
Yogurt:
    and calories, 152
    as low-fat alternative ingredient,
        19, 50, 152–53, 164–65
    dressing, creamy, romaine with,
        116

Yogurt—*continued*
    frozen, apple flakes with, 139
    frozen, caramel cups with, **159,**
        172–73
    in honey sauce for blackberries,
        151
    sauce, spicy, grilled swordfish
        with, 49

Z

Ziti (tubular pasta) and vegetables,
    gratin of, *10,* 36–37
Zucchini:
    "boats," stuffed, with red
        pepper–tomato sauce, *7,*
        78–79
    and tomato fans, *13,* **26,** 29

Page numbers in *italic* designate the menu that includes the dish; those in **bold** designate the photograph of the dish.

SUPPORT YOUR LOCAL PUBLIC BROADCASTING STATION!

KQED is governed by an elected, volunteer board of directors. These dedicated citizens plan the station's direction and work with the professional staff and the hundreds of thousands of loyal members to bring the highest quality television, radio, and print programming to local audiences. We gratefully salute these members of the KQED Board of Directors:

Edward M. Allen, Anne C. Broome, Lyn Chan, E. Michael Darby, MD, Lois M. DeDomenico, Rosemarie Fernandez-Ruel, Stanley J. Friedman, Sasha Futran, William D. Glenn, Charlene C. Harvey (Chair), Thomas Hsieh, Jr., John H. Jacobs, Shelley A. Kessler, Henry M. Kroll, Marian E. Lever, Cynthia C. Magowan, Jerry W. Mapp, Leo P. Martinez, Robert B. Philipp, Mary Camblin Reed, Jonathan C. Rice, Sylvia M. Siegel, Kenneth H. Simmons, Sherry H. Smith, Leo C. Soong, William G. Toland III, Stephen N. Worthington.

And we recognize the dedicated contributions of the boards and staff of our 346 sister stations throughout the PBS network.

Every community across America is reached by one of the 346 member stations of the Public Broadcasting Service. These stations bring information, entertainment, and insight to the whole family.

Think about the programs you enjoy and remember most:

Mystery . . . Masterpiece Theatre . . . Nova . . . Nature . . . Sesame Street . . . Ghostwriter . . . Reading Rainbow . . . "I'll Fly Away" . . . MacNeil/Lehrer News Hour . . . Great Performances . . . National Geographic . . . American Playhouse . . . and so many more.

On your local PBS station, you'll also find fascinating adult education courses, provocative documentaries, great cooking and do-it-yourself programs, and thoughtful local analysis.

Many public television series—like *Today's Gourmet with Jacques Pépin*—are underwritten by generous corporate citizens such as those recognized here. But more than half of all public television budgets come from individual member support.

For less than the cost of a night at the movies, less than a couple of months of a daily paper, less than a month of your cable TV bill, you can help make possible all the quality programming you enjoy.

Become a member of your public broadcasting station and do your part.

Public Television. You make it happen!

ENJOY *ALL* THE SCRUMPTIOUS DISHES
FROM *TODAY'S GOURMET!*

All the healthy, taste-tempting recipes from the first two seasons of *Today's Gourmet* are available in their companion cookbooks, *Today's Gourmet* and *Good Life Cooking.* Each book contains more than 100 recipes marked by Jacques's characteristic imagination and devotion to sharing good food with family and friends.

$15.95 each at your favorite bookstore.

Or call 1–800–441–3000.

Happy Cooking!

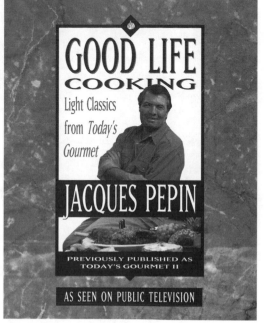

PRODUCTION OF THE PUBLIC TELEVISION SERIES
TODAY'S GOURMET WITH JACQUES PÉPIN
IS MADE POSSIBLE BY GENEROUS GRANTS FROM

BRAUN
Designed to perform better.

Cambria

········ ESTATE ······ BOTTLED ········

WORLD CLASS WINES FROM CALIFORNIA'S SANTA MARIA VALLEY

RUSSELL RANGE

THE *ELEGANT* PROFESSIONAL